The concept for the exhibition and book was born out of Warren Coville's love of photography and his passion for work by photographers of the Clarence White School. Convinced as he is that White equaled Stieglitz in influencing subsequent generations of artists—and, perhaps, surpassed him in promoting the medium as an art—Coville became a collector of White's work and of those who attended his school.

The transformation of pictorialist ideals into modernist aesthetics as revealed by the philosophy and teachings of Clarence H. White constitutes the essence of this book and exhibition. To Warren Coville, whose exceptional generosity has enabled a wider audience to share the quality of his own discoveries, and to all those who contributed in so many ways to this project, we offer our gratitude.

JAMES L. ENYEART
Director, George Eastman House

SAMUEL SACHS II
Director, Detroit Institute of Arts

HOW COLLECTING BECOMES A PASSION   *Warren J. Coville*

In 1974 while visiting some friends in Washington, D.C., I saw an Ansel Adams exhibit. I was captured by the beauty of the images, but I had to overcome the psychological hurdle of spending $350 for one photograph. After much deliberation I made the purchase. With that step, my awakening interest grew, slowly at first, into a passion as I learned about the history and the artists of photography.

Although initially I had not developed a theme for my collection, I had read in depth about those photographers whose work I collected. By 1980 I had committed my interest to photographers and works of the Photo-Secession. Thomas Halsted, of the Halsted Gallery in Birmingham, Michigan, brought to my attention a group of nine photographs, a portfolio by Clarence H. White that was for sale at Sotheby's. Tom was the successful bidder on my behalf, and thus started a much deeper interest in White. As I read material on White, I became aware of the Clarence H. White School of Photography, although there was very little written about it.

In 1988 I increased my collecting of works by White's students. By 1990 the collection had grown to more than 1500 pieces. Although I had kept it well documented, maintaining the documentation was becoming time-consuming. In 1992 I hired Kathleen A. Erwin as curator of the collection. I knew Kathy from when I was a volunteer at the Detroit Institute of Arts, where she worked for many years in the Graphic Arts Department.

When Kathy became familiar with the collection, we discussed the possibility of a Clarence H. White School exhibition. Once there was the idea for a show, many questions came to mind: When did White start the school? What were the courses? Who were the teachers and who were the students? What was White's influence? The work of photographers such as Outerbridge, Steiner, Ulmann, Lange, and Bourke-White was so different from his, yet they were his students. How could a photographer so entrenched in the Photo-Secession and in the pictorialist tradition have such an imaginative student body whose work differed so much from his own? We recognized that no one had researched the school in depth and that we wanted to know more.

Kathy's research uncovered much new information and led to the documenting of most of the school's important students; her work proved to be a steady guide to enhancing the collection even further. An example of this is Margaret Watkins, a student, teacher, and successful photographer of the White School. Her story sparked my wife, Margot, and me to go to Glasgow, Scotland, to visit Joseph Mulholland, Watkins's trusted friend and neighbor. The experience of sitting across the street from where Watkins had lived and sharing with Mulholland the unique relationship he had had with her, and viewing the wonderful photographic images she had left to him, was a great reward for my commitment to this project.

In the fall 1983 issue of *Studies in Visual Communication*, there was an article, "Clarence H. White Reconsidered: An Alternative to the Modernist Aesthetic of Straight Photography," by Bonnie Yochelson. After reading this article, it was evident to me that Yochelson shared many of my thoughts about White. I invited her to contribute to this book; her essay clearly spells out White's involvement, not only with his school, but with the Art Center and the Pictorial Photographers of America as well.

Clarence H. White was without a doubt one of the most important figures in American photography following the demise of the Photo-Secession; his influence as a teacher continued for a number of years after his death. While White's teaching affected each of his students, in no way did he encourage them to copy his style. Instead, he fostered individuality in his students' work. His focus on design and composition aimed at not just art photography, but extended to commercial work and portraiture as well.

White has already earned recognition as a great photographer of the Photo-Secession period. He also deserves recognition as a great teacher. His passion was to create a universal appreciation of art and design. Although he did not achieve this goal—and it would be an unrealistic expectation for anyone—his efforts brought about a much larger circle of artistically knowledge-able individuals. In a review of the *Clarence H. White Memorial Exhibition*, published in the May 1926 issue of *The Photo Miniature*, Margaret Watkins is quoted: "He used himself to serve his art, and not his art to serve himself."

My passion for collecting has motivated me to better understand Clarence H. White, and I believe he should be recognized as the preeminent American who has influenced photographers and graphic artists in all artistic disciplines. I hope that this book and the accompanying exhibition will help to make his significance even more evident.

CLARENCE H. WHITE

PEACEFUL WARRIOR

Bonnie Yochelson

IN 1923, TWO YEARS BEFORE HIS UNTIMELY DEATH AT THE AGE OF FIFTY-FOUR, CLARENCE H. WHITE SUMMED UP HIS CAREER:

I took up photography, as nine out of ten of the photographers do, as a hobby, and pursued it with all the enthusiasm of the amateur; so much so that a change of occupation became necessary. Photography then became my real work, but [I] still was anxious to keep the attitude of the amateur, doing the best in me, believing in photography as an expression for the artist. This persistence led me into another field of photography, that of teaching. . . . I still have a thrill when I think I am on the right road, and a little envy when I see a beginner who appears to have arrived.[1]

As a young man in Newark, Ohio, in the 1890s, White was a beginner who arrived with a vengeance. He produced a body of photographs that, according to one critic, brought the world to Newark.[2] In 1906, at the age of thirty-five, White moved to New York City and soon began a teaching career there. From the outset, White himself was concerned that teaching might infringe upon his art. In a 1908 letter to fellow pictorialist F. Holland Day, he confessed, "I hate . . . to look to the future and see myself a dried up teacher of photography."[3] White's work suffered in his later years, but his natural gifts as a teacher blossomed, and many of his students went on to pioneer the new advertising photography that developed into a full-fledged industry in the 1930s.

The decline in White's output led colleagues to regret his career change,[4] and the seeming disparity between White's own lyrical pictorialism and the fashionable modernism of many of his best students, including Anton Bruehl, Paul Outerbridge Jr., Ralph Steiner, and Margaret Watkins, has baffled historians.[5] White's achievements as a teacher, however, leave no cause for remorse or confusion. His vision of photography's future was prophetic; his social and aesthetic philosophy was consistent; and his program for training young photographers, which extended far beyond the classroom, was highly effective.

When White set out to earn his living by photography, he maintained the idealistic belief that society could well use the services of a photographic artist. Indeed, it was upon this premise that he built his teaching career. Alert to the possibilities of photographic illustration, White taught not only photography but modern art and print-making at the Clarence H. White School of Photography, which he opened in New York City in 1914. As the founding president in 1917 of the Pictorial Photographers of America, he provided a bridge between the older amateurs of the photographic societies and a younger generation of professionally oriented art photographers. And, with the opening of the Art Center in 1921, which he helped establish, White collaborated with art directors, publishers, and graphic designers who, like him, were seeking to define the artist's role in the communications revolution of the 1920s.

By the time of his death in 1925, White had succeeded in establishing an institutional network to support the artistic and professional ambitions of his students. The 1920s were a heady time, when an avowed socialist like White could join forces with a corporate giant like Condé Nast Publications in the name of art. That moment passed with the Depression, which deflated the artistic pretensions of publishers, focusing their attention on the bottom line, and marked the collapse of the delicate balance of art and commerce for which White had worked tirelessly and in which he had placed his hopes.

AMATEUR OR PROFESSIONAL, 1896–1906

As a teenager, White had wanted to be a painter, but after graduating from high school in 1890, he opted to follow his father into the wholesale grocery firm of Fleek and Neal. A trip on his honeymoon to the 1893 Chicago Columbian Exposition gave White his first opportunity to see contemporary art and prompted him to take up the camera. He began exhibiting his photographs in 1897, and his work was immediately recognized by painters and photographers as new and compelling.[6]

In his carefully composed and subtly lit genre scenes of family and friends, White exhibited a full understanding of the artistic currents of his day, from Whistler and Japanese prints to art nouveau and impressionism. That such artistically sophisticated work was created by one so young and apparently provincial can be explained, in part, by the wide range of magazines to which White subscribed, including not only photography journals and popular weeklies, but also American and European art magazines such as *Magazine of Art, Jugend,* and *Arts et Decoration.* The black-and-white engravings that illustrated these journals may have provided clearer compositional models for White's black-and-white photographs than did the few original paintings that were available to him; for example, it was most likely from a magazine illustration that White modeled his 1899 *Ring Toss,* based on William Merritt Chase's 1896 version of the same theme.[7]

White's art was also fed by the small but international band of pictorial photographers, who as early as 1898 embraced him. Through exhibitions and publications, White became familiar with English, French, and German pictorialism, and established friendships with such luminaries as Alfred Stieglitz and Gertrude Käsebier from New York, and F. Holland Day and Alvin Langdon Coburn from Boston. White was responsible for drawing into this fold Edward Steichen, then a young, unknown lithographer's assistant from Milwaukee. Images by these photographers resonate with common themes and motifs, as a comparison of White's *The Bashful Child* and Käsebier's *Blessed Art Thou Among Women*, both of 1899, demonstrates.[8]

White's Ohio photographs struck a deeper emotional chord than most of the work produced by his celebrated colleagues. Like so many introspective artists of his generation, from the pre-Raphaelite Dante Gabriel Rossetti to the Belgian symbolist Ferdinand Khnopff, White obsessively studied the women in his life to give form to his reflections on the nature of physical and spiritual beauty. With his wife, Jane, and her three sisters as muses, White created what Peter Bunnell has aptly called a "private epic."[9] This commitment to a personal vision was what White described simply as "doing the best in me" and was what he hoped to elicit in later years from his students.

Closer to home, White found an articulate supporter in Ohio-born artist O. Walter Beck. Trained in Munich, Beck was a fashionable academic painter and teacher of composition who espoused the orientalist aesthetics of Ernest F. Fenollosa, the nation's leading authority on Japanese art. Beck was convinced that Americans' attitudes toward art were too literal and that conventional photography, which strove to imitate nature, aggravated this shortcoming. He argued that "artistic photography" was "the art of the people" and defended work that, like White's, "express[ed] feeling through . . . arrangement." In 1904 Beck organized an exhibition of White's photographs at the Pratt Institute in Brooklyn, where he had begun teaching a few years earlier. Beck's manual of 1907, *Art Principles in Portrait Photography*, presented a step-by-step approach to composition that was illustrated with photographs inferior to White's; nevertheless, Beck's belief that "art *can* be brought into photography and it *can* be taught!" (emphasis Beck's) gave voice to White's convictions.[10]

Beck shared with White the ideals of the American arts and crafts movement, which inspired White's approach to his art and teaching. Derived from the English critique of modern industry's demeaning working conditions in factories and shoddily produced wares, the movement affirmed the dignity of labor and the importance of beauty in everyday living. For arts and crafts advocates, the enrichment of the lives of ordinary people took many forms, from the manufacture of quality goods according to socialist

labor practices, to art education for the general public, through the exhibitions and publications of amateur craft societies. As guardians of the home, women figured prominently in the arts and crafts cause and played an especially active role in its societies.

Pictorial photography, which sought to elevate a mechanized and commercialized craft to the status of art, shared many of the principles and practices of the arts and crafts movement.[11] More than most pictorial photographers, White adopted its ideals. His photographs of the harmonious relationships between women and children in domestic and natural surroundings depict the arts and crafts way of life. The Newark Camera Club, which White founded in 1898 and which included many women, treated with equal respect the efforts of local members and national leaders. In 1899 White organized a Newark Camera Club exhibition that toured Cincinnati, New York, Philadelphia, and Washington. One critic characterized the club's work as "the most helpful means in the world for the artistic education of the layman."[12]

White's interest in photographic illustration, at a time when photomechanical reproduction was still in its infancy, also derived from arts and crafts ideals. Because magazine illustration had provided the foundation for his own artistic education, White understood the edifying value of high-quality reproductions in the popular press. By 1904 he had illustrated Irving Bacheller's book *Eben Holden* and Ira Billman's *Songs of All Seasons*, as well as Clara Morris's story "Beneath the Wrinkle" in *McClure's Magazine*. Stieglitz chose the finest of these works, rural genre scenes from *Eben Holden*, for reproduction as photogravures in his exquisitely printed journal *Camera Work*.[13] Partly because of these reproductions, White became well known in photography circles as an illustrator. In a 1904 article, "Aesthetic Activity in Photography," critic Sadakichi Hartmann noted that White "saw in photography a medium for serious, high-class book and magazine illustration."[14] The next year, French pictorial photographer Robert Demachy reproduced six White photographs in an article in *La Revue de Photographie* (vol. 3, no. 11 [1905]) on magazine illustration. And White's close friendship with Boston pictorialist F. Holland Day, joint owner of the influential arts and crafts publishing firm of Copeland and Day, was nurtured by their mutual interest in fine art printing and photographic illustration.

White's decision in 1904 to leave Fleek and Neal for a career as a photographer expressed his ultimate faith in arts and crafts ideology. Liberated from a job that he had held for fourteen years but never enjoyed, White hoped to support his family without compromising his art. Although many pictorialists—especially Stieglitz—clung to amateurism as an exemption from the profit motive and therefore as a badge of integrity, White chose an alternative route. He wagered his future on the belief that art and social usefulness were compatible.

For two years after leaving the grocery business, White traveled widely to complete commissions for portraits and commercial illustration. The high point of White's journeys was his visits to the "Old Red House," the home of Steven and Jean Reynolds in Terre Haute, Indiana. Ten of White's photographs of the Reynolds family, which he gathered into a portfolio containing about fifty images, were published in 1906 by George Bicknell in *The Craftsman* (vol. 9), the leading journal of the American arts and crafts movement. These portraits of Steven, Jean, and their three children present a world of haunting beauty equaling that of White's photographs of his own family (page 19). In the Reynolds portraits, White found the unity of artistic and professional purpose that he had hoped was possible.

White's sojourns at the Old Red House also led him to embrace socialism. Reynolds was a wealthy lawyer who served as campaign manager to Eugene Debs, the American Socialist Party's three-time candidate for president of the United States. Among the "Soapbox Travellers and Apostles of Truth" that "found shelter and food and repaired their raiment"[15] at the Old Red House were the lawyer Clarence Darrow, who represented Debs, and Horace Traubel, Walt Whitman's friend and biographer. White's relationships with members of the Red House Salon were not superficial. Inscribing a copy of his 1908 biography of Eugene Debs, Stephen Reynolds wrote to White: "To My loved Comrade Brother who knows our Dear Gene and who will appreciate this work of love." White maintained a friendship with Horace Traubel until Traubel's death in 1919 and provided a portrait of Traubel for his book of poems, *Optimos*; Clarence Darrow solicited White to illustrate a book (the commission never materialized).[16] The ideology of the Old Red House, however, was more firmly rooted in Whitman's paeans to the working man than in Karl Marx's class conflict. According to Peter Bunnell (*Reverence*, 12), one of White's favorite books was Edward Carpenter's *Towards Democracy* (1883), a series of Whitmanesque poems celebrating the life of the common laborer. Carpenter was, in fact, a disciple of Whitman, and was widely read before World War I, then quickly fell into obscurity. This romantic socialism, consistent with that of William Morris, the founder of the English arts and crafts movement, reaffirmed White's social and aesthetic ideals.[17]

Although White's experiment as a traveling photographer was an artistic and financial success, it strained his family life. In 1906 White moved to New York City; his wife, two older sons, and newborn son followed the next year. The decision to move to New York, which suffered no shortage of professional photographers, was a measure of White's ambitions. Part of the city's lure was the presence of Stieglitz, who, by forming the elite Photo-Secession in 1902 and opening the Little Galleries of the Photo-Secession in 1905, had assumed the leadership of American pictorial photography. New York also offered White a larger cultural arena in which to explore his ambitious aesthetic philosophy.

CLARENCE H. WHITE

The Kiss (The Reynolds Sisters), 1904

23

WYNN RICHARDS

Woman in Shower, ca. 1932

PAUL OUTERBRIDGE JR.

Nude Female Sitting at Dressing Table, ca. 1936

SETTLING IN NEW YORK: 1906–1912

Perhaps seeking to soften the contrast between small-town Newark and downtown New York, White moved his family to the hilly, semi-rural neighborhood of Morningside Heights in northern Manhattan. From 1906 to 1912 he rented an apartment on Claremont Avenue, a quiet street with a view overlooking the Hudson River. The neighborhood was swiftly becoming an urban Parnassus, with grand institutions of higher learning springing up overnight: a few blocks southeast, the campuses of Columbia University and Barnard College were nearing completion; the Union Theological Seminary and the Juilliard School of Music were under construction to the south; and the new campus of City College rose several blocks to the northeast. The opening of the subway in 1904 had stimulated this new construction, and now allowed White to commute in twenty minutes to his studio on Union Square, in the heart of the city's commercial and cultural district.

In 1908 White moved his studio north to 5 West 31st Street, a townhouse recently vacated by the Camera Club of New York, where he had been an active member until 1907, when Stieglitz was ousted.[18] Just off Fifth Avenue, the new studio was part of the fashionable district between 23rd and 59th Streets, which a commentator in *Abel's Photographic Weekly* (16 January 1909, 74–75) called "the photographer's metropolis." Around the corner at 291 Fifth Avenue was Stieglitz's Little Galleries of the Photo-Secession (called "291"), and three blocks north was the studio of fellow Photo-Secessionist Gertrude Käsebier. The neighborhood was also home to the city's art galleries, which White frequented.[19]

White took great pains to decorate his studio, which was not only a work space but a showcase for clients. Its light brown walls, green hangings, old Franklin stove, Japanese prints, Chinese pottery, and bamboo window screens were an arts and crafts proclamation. He described the studio as "very simple" and "quiet," an effect that was expressive of his own modest personality.[20]

Like other Photo-Secessionists, such as Käsebier, Steichen, and Coburn, White concentrated on portrait commissions to earn his living. As Jane White later explained, her husband's approach to this "bread-and-butter" work was anything but routine:

> Clarence White's soul suffered many rebellions — & much as he needed money he would refuse to do the portrait of a person for whom he felt no spontaneous sympathy. That was his privilege unquestionably.[21]

White also sought illustration commissions but completed only two for popular magazines, one on Newport summer houses for *Everybody's Magazine* in 1908 and one on the actress Maude Adams for *Burr McIntosh Monthly* in 1909. In 1911 he agonized to

complete a Barnard College calendar (fig. 1), and in 1912 he began accepting advertising assignments, an innovation in photographic illustration.[22]

White's commissioned photographs were often worthy of his talent, but he never again developed a body of work comparable to the Reynolds portfolio. Almost as soon as he had set up his studio, White's attention was diverted to teaching; his letters bear witness to his inability to find enough time for independent work. Instead, White began to encourage his students to follow a path that he never wholeheartedly pursued himself.

In 1907 White was asked to teach an evening course at Columbia University's Teachers College, which happened to be conveniently located three blocks from his home. The offer came from Arthur Wesley Dow, who had assumed the chair of the college's fine arts department three years earlier. Although Dow had originally offered the job to Stieglitz, who in turn recommended White,[23] Dow already knew of White and his work. Before he arrived at Teachers College, Dow had taught at Pratt, where he knew Beck, and among Dow's former students were White's friends Käsebier and Coburn. A nationally prominent art educator who was fourteen years White's senior, Dow was a natural mentor for White, whose formal education had ended with high school and whose previous teaching experience was limited to a few lectures at arts and crafts clubs. White remained on the college faculty until his death.[24]

Dow was an accomplished printmaker and amateur photographer who had studied painting in Boston, Paris, and the Pont-Aven artist colony in Brittany. Trained by Ernest Fenollosa at the Museum of Fine Arts, Boston, Dow had also become a leading expert on Japanese prints.[25] Dow's textbook *Composition*, first published in 1899, codified Fenollosa's art theory, which wedded Eastern and Western art principles and asserted the expressive value of formal qualities, such as spatial arrangement and tonal variation. Drawing on a wide range of examples from the history of art, Dow isolated design principles, such as repetition, symmetry, and opposition, which he hoped would form the basis of a national art and elevate public taste. White was familiar with Fenollosa's ideas through Beck, but Dow provided White with a more fully articulated theory and more sophisticated and wide-ranging artistic models.

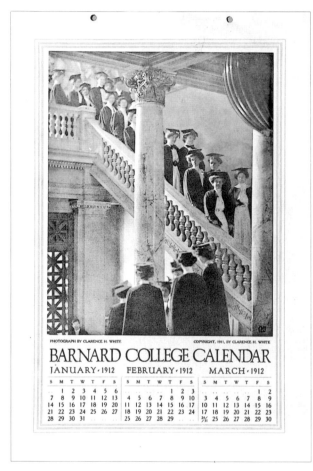

(figure 1)

CLARENCE H. WHITE
*Barnard College Calendar,
January–March 1912*

Dow's art theory also drew heavily on the arts and crafts critique of the separation of fine and utilitarian art. Rather than teach fine artists to imitate nature and craftsmen to imitate decorative patterns, Dow insisted that all art students master a set of principles applicable to all art forms, from furniture and fabrics to painting and sculpture. Having mastered these principles, a student could employ them meaningfully, not mechanically. Dow considered this training a form of empowerment for art producer and consumer alike. His philosophy, true to arts and crafts ideals, intertwined the concepts of power, freedom, and efficiency:

> A training that calls for a very direct exercise of the critical powers, developing judgment and skill, is a training that will increase the individual's efficiency whatever his calling may be. . . . A better understanding of the true usefulness of art recognizes creative power as a divine gift, the natural endowment of every human soul. . . . It is the individual's right to have full control of these powers.[26]

The fact that Dow found a place for pictorial photography in his utilitarian theory of art fortified White's belief that photographers could find a productive use for their art.[27]

When White was hired by Teachers College, he entered the eye of a storm over educational reform.[28] Under the deanship of James Earl Russell, Teachers College was the nation's leading force in progressive education. Inspired by Columbia philosopher John Dewey, the college's faculty was more than a group of teachers' teachers. They were proselytizers for a philosophy of education with urgent political implications. They believed that the citizenry of a stable democracy must be capable of purposeful thinking and that education must be active and experimental, not passive and imitative. Central to their philosophy was Dewey's "project method," which asked students to solve problems derived from their immediate experience rather than master a roster of required subjects.[29]

That White would later describe the instruction at his own school as "the project method" was not coincidental. Like Dewey, White used his students' immediate environment and emphasized problem-solving experiments rather than "content." Dorothea Lange, who studied with White in 1917, recalled a typical assignment:

> The assignment was generally to go out to a certain place—oh, something like . . . a wrought iron gate, nothing better than that, something that you'd never really look at, just be kind of aware of some curly-ques there, an undistinguished thing—and photograph that thing! . . . It was close by, and it was handy, so he sent these students there. . . . Oh, I was aware, dimly, that there was some kind of underlying wisdom in the man that would choose this utterly banal thing, around which, or through which, he could guide them instead of telling them to photograph more flowery or more romantic things.[30]

ANTOINETTE B. HERVEY

In the Arbor, by 1919

White worked to publish the best of these assignments in school brochures, calendars, and newspapers, showing that the project method could yield utilitarian results. The large number of student works depicting the area around Columbia University are evidence of this method. In 1920, the university produced a lavish souvenir, *Columbia University, Photographic Studies*, which reproduced eighteen full-page photographs by White students. After opening his own school, White encouraged his students to photograph its classrooms and exterior; examples illustrated the school's brochures.

White, like Dewey, also believed that a teacher's goal was not to impart the "right" answer but to lead his students to self-discovery. Lange's reflection on White's criticism reveals this pedagogical approach.

> He would and did accept everything. He was most uncritical. He always saw the print in relation to the person and then he would start to stammer and writhe around. But the point is that he gave everyone some feeling of encouragement in some peculiar way. You walked into that dreary room knowing that something was going to happen. Now what happened I don't know, but you never forgot it. I can hear his voice still.[31]

Such testimonials have often been cited as evidence of White's gentle soul. White's teaching style, however, owes as much to his educational philosophy as to his temperament.

In 1908 White accepted a second teaching position, at the Brooklyn Institute of Arts and Sciences, where he remained on the faculty until 1922. Opened as the Apprentice's Library in 1823, the institute was the hub of Brooklyn's cultural activities. Between 1888 and 1907 it embarked on a building program that included the Brooklyn Museum, the Academy of Music, the Botanic Garden, and the nation's first Children's Museum. In 1889 the institute established one of the first departments of photography in the country. The department's classroom and darkroom were located in the newly constructed Academy of Music, which was conveniently located on the subway line from Manhattan to Brooklyn, a line that opened the same year White began teaching at the institute.[32]

The dramatic growth of Columbia Teachers College and the Brooklyn Institute, as well as Pratt Institute, City College, and Brooklyn College, was a response to the huge swell of European immigrants who arrived in New York from the 1880s until World War I. These immigrants advanced the city's economy but disturbed its status quo, and enlightened public opinion decreed that education should speed their assimilation into American life. White's teaching appointments connected him to these institutions as they carried out their mandate of bringing technical training and cultural enrichment to a vast new public.

White opened his own school for a less high-minded purpose: to solve the problem of summers in New York City. As early as June 1907 he considered buying an

"interesting old house going to rack" on Long Island.[33] In 1908 and 1909 he took his family to F. Holland Day's "Castle Guiney" on Georgetown Island, Maine, a site that Jane White called "the promised land." In 1910 White purchased a neglected farmhouse near Day's home for $100 and opened a summer school, named the Seguinland School of Photography. Students boarded at the nearby Seguinland Hotel; a neighboring cottage became a studio and darkroom; and Day, Käsebier, and Max Weber came to critique student work. This "working vacation" allowed the Whites to enjoy an upper-middle-class luxury that they could not otherwise afford.[34] In 1916 White moved the summer school to East Canaan, Connecticut, within two hours' drive of New York City; the following year, he moved the summer school to nearby Canaan, where it remained until his death in 1925.

Although many summer schools attracted wealthy women of little apparent seriousness, White's school offered a substantive program for motivated photographers. Arthur Chapman, one of White's most talented early students, wrote about the first summer:

> To begin with, there was the class itself. It had come from the four corners of the earth and all points West, thus—a man from Ecuador; a professional woman photographer from California, and another from Baltimore, who lived much abroad; a college professor from Philadelphia; an advertising man from New York and Chicago; a globe-trotter from everywhere—Egypt mostly; a librarian from Chicago; a stenographer from New York. Mixing with a crowd like that will take the artistic nonsense out of anybody. Apprentices, journeyman, amateurs and professionals exchanged prejudices, and discovered that whoever said there was only one right way to do a thing was an unmitigated liar. The beginners learned that the professionals and journeyman amateurs didn't know such a helava-lot after all, and it was a terrific shock to the latter to discover that the apprentice, in brassy disregard of custom and precedent, insisted on producing good pictures.[35]

White's summer workshop was the forerunner of the Clarence H. White School of Photography, which opened in Manhattan in 1914. White's most distinguished pupil in these early years was Karl Struss, who attended evening classes at Columbia from 1908 to 1912. Struss's background recalled White's own. Following his father's wishes, Struss worked for eleven years in the family's bonnet wire factory while establishing a reputation in amateur photography. In 1910 his work was featured in Stieglitz's prestigious and controversial exhibition at the Albright Gallery in Buffalo, and he was named to the Photo-Secession; in 1912 eight of his photographs appeared in *Camera Work*.

Unlike White, however, Struss did not begin his photography career in a cultural backwater. He spent the summer of 1909 photographing in Europe and upon his return became close to Stieglitz, Coburn, and Weber. Most important, Struss had White as a mentor. In 1912 White sponsored a one-man show of Struss's work at Teachers College,

CLARENCE H. WHITE

Karl Struss, 1912

enlisted Struss to teach his college summer school course, and recommended Struss to carry on with the Barnard calendar commission. When White opened his Manhattan school in 1914, he gave Struss the lease to his 31st Street studio. In 1916 White asked Struss to help teach his course and arrange the annual photography exhibition at the Brooklyn Institute. Walking in White's footsteps, Struss developed a thriving commercial practice as a pioneer magazine photographer and began fulfilling the goals White had set for himself as a photographic illustrator.

Struss, like White, preferred a soft-focus lens and platinum printing paper, and he valued White for his "great sense of composition."[36] But Struss photographed the streets of New York, a subject foreign to White. Along with Coburn, Weber, Stieglitz, and Paul Haviland (another White student),[37] Struss explored the modern city with an eye to unconventional compositional ideas. Between 1909 and 1915 he produced a massive portrait of New York that included startling images, such as *Queensboro Bridge,* that approach pure abstraction (page 41). White instilled in Struss a sense of picture construction without limiting his artistic freedom and created opportunities for him to exhibit, teach, and sell.[38] It was a role that White would perform for his best students throughout his years as a teacher. Struss ultimately broke with White during World War I, and abandoned New York for Hollywood.

Struss was the only student to benefit from the support of both White and Stieglitz, who enjoyed a close working relationship with White during White's first years in New York. In 1906–7 White had helped run the Photo-Secession gallery and had supervised the printing of *Camera Work.*[39] In 1907 they had collaborated on a series of experimental nudes and had shared the "color fever" for the new autochrome process.[40] It was in the spirit of fellowship that White had moved his studio from Union Square to 31st Street and Fifth Avenue, around the corner from 291.

But proximity brought tensions. Soon after White's arrival, Käsebier felt White snubbed her. Käsebier then fought with Stieglitz over a review of her work printed in *Camera Work.* Käsebier and White both resented the growing intimacy between Stieglitz and Steichen.[41] In a letter to Day, White complained, "I blame Fifth Avenue for much. The devil will get anyone that stays on it long enough."[42] The final dissolution of the Photo-Secession came in the wake of the 1910 Albright Gallery exhibition at Buffalo, organized by Stieglitz. Disputes over payments and unreturned prints veiled deeper dissatisfactions with Stieglitz's unyielding domination of the group at a time when his enthusiasm for pictorial photography was waning. White, Käsebier, and Coburn all defected, but it was White, with his young band of aspiring photographers in tow, who led the effort to promote pictorial photography without Stieglitz.[43] He was

joined by Weber, who had designed the Buffalo exhibition and endured a humiliating rift with Stieglitz during the 1911 exhibition of his paintings at 291.

The new group's earliest efforts were exhibitions intended to show high-quality work free of Stieglitz's offensive elitism. The first exhibition, at the Free Public Library of Newark, New Jersey, in the spring of 1911, was sponsored by the Newark Museum Association; like the Buffalo exhibition of 1910, it was hung by Weber. The exhibit's inclusion of Photo-Secessionists, "other well-known pictorialists," and White students from Teachers College and the Brooklyn Institute violated Photo-Secessionist policy, which had required members to exhibit as a separate group.[44]

In October 1912 White organized a more ambitious exhibition "illustrating the progress of the art of photography in America" at the Montross Art Galleries on Fifth Avenue.[45] The Montross, which featured American impressionist paintings and regularly showed Dow's work, was a congenial locale for pictorial photography.[46] Like the Newark exhibition, the Montross show combined photographs by White's students with works by accomplished pictorialists, including the Photo-Pictorialists of Buffalo, who had boycotted the Buffalo exhibition in 1910. White even tried to solicit work from Stieglitz but was unsuccessful.[47]

With 291 off limits, White and his colleagues gravitated to a more hospitable gathering place, The Little Book-shop Around the Corner at 2 East 29th Street. Opened by Mitchell Kennerley in 1907, the shop was named for the Little Church Around the Corner, across 29th Street at the corner of Fifth Avenue.[48] Kennerley was a gifted publisher whose literary discoveries included Edna St. Vincent Millay, Van Wyck Brooks, Sinclair Lewis, and Walter Lippmann. Unlike the large retail bookstores along Fifth Avenue, the Little Book-shop catered to the noncommercial tastes of Kennerley's authors and their friends who congregated there. In 1910 Kennerley sold the shop to his manager, Laurence Gomme, who welcomed White's group into the fold.

White's new alliance came through Coburn, the typographer Frederic W. Goudy, and the critic Temple Scott. In 1911 Kennerley published a book of short stories by H. G. Wells, illustrated with photogravures by Coburn.[49] The book was designed and printed by Goudy, who had set up his workshop in the back of Kennerley's store after his own office burned in 1908.[50] White and Goudy first worked together in 1911 when Goudy printed White's 1912 Barnard calendar.

White's relationship with the omnipresent Scott had several sources. White probably knew Scott through Stieglitz, who had published Scott in *Camera Work*.[51] Scott had featured his friend Weber in a 1910 parody, published by Kennerley, of Stieglitz's Holland House dinners.[52] A Little Book-shop regular, Scott also had a friendship with Goudy,

KARL STRUSS
New York Harbor, East River, 1909

CLARA E. SIPPRELL
Tents and Clouds at the Hill Camp,
Hanoum Camps, Thetford, Vermont, 1917

KARL STRUSS
The Landing Place, Villa Carlotta, Lake
Como, Italy, 1909

1909

whom he praised as a "true craftsman of today" in a 1912 essay published by a White student.[53] By October 1912 White had enlisted the services of Goudy and Scott for his group: Goudy designed the Montross exhibition catalogue, and Scott wrote its introductory essay.

At the Little Book-shop, Goudy and Scott brought White into contact with New York's publishing world. Increasingly, the shop became home to pictorial photographers, with a section of photography books on its shelves and a permanent exhibition of photographs by White, Steichen, Coburn, and other "exponents of th[e] new movement" on its walls.[54] By the end of 1914 White's group met bimonthly at the bookstore to show lantern slides and prints and to hear Weber offer criticism.[55] The group lost this congenial meetingplace in 1917, when Gomme closed the shop and joined the war effort.

A PROGRAM EVOLVES: 1913–1919

From the Little Book-shop Around the Corner, White's group published *Platinum Print* (renamed *Photo=Graphic Art* in 1916).[56] Although listed on the journal's masthead as an associate, White was *Platinum Print's* guiding spirit. The journal was a labor of love, however, for Edward R. Dickson, a devoted White student, who served as its editor and publisher.[57] Coburn was its foreign correspondent, and the other associates, including Struss and Goudy, were all White intimates.[58]

Platinum Print was "designed to take a place between *Camera Work* and the periodicals devoted to the less advanced photographer,"[59] with emphasis on "the entrance of the pictorialist in the field of illustrative art (1913, vol. 1, no. 1, p. 13)." Designed and printed by Goudy, it contained high-quality halftone illustrations. Issues opened with poems by contemporary authors Estelle Duclos, Ernest Dowson, Maurice Baring, James Stephens, Edward H. Pfeiffer, Salomon de la Selva, Rabindranath Tagore, and Chuang Tzu; most were already well published, and some may have belonged to the Little Book-shop crowd. Articles addressed artistic, not technical matters. Weber and Scott regularly contributed essays on aesthetics, Dickson offered stylistic analyses of Japanese prints, and Goudy contributed "Typographica," a regular column on the history of lettering. The group's exhibitions received extensive review, and the "Photographic Activities" column reported events at the bookshop, Teachers College, and the Brooklyn Institute.

Reflecting White's teaching, Dickson's editorials urged photographers to gain "the ability to see vividly" and to eschew "the conventional landscapes and profiles now unfortunately encountered at so many exhibitions." Dickson encouraged photographers to study other arts, visit exhibitions "with open eyes," and aim for "the conversion of the commonplace into the beautiful (*Platinum Print*, vol. 1, no. 5)." Regrettably,

EDWARD R. DICKSON

Design in Nature, ca. 1913

Platinum Print never fulfilled its ambitious publication schedule of seven issues each year. Only in its first year did it run with reasonable regularity and attract substantial advertising. In Gomme's words, "Th[e] magazine end[ed] for precisely the same reason it began, namely, lack of funds."[60]

Although its publication waned, the group's exhibition activities continued apace, reaching out to old Photo-Secessionists and their rivals alike. In January 1914 White arranged an international exhibition of pictorial photography at the Ehrich Art Galleries at 707 Fifth Avenue. The gallery, which was owned by Walter L. Ehrich, whose wife, Adelaide, was one of White's students, specialized in old-master prints. European photography was well represented, with prints by Frederick Evans, George Davison, Baron Adolph de Meyer, Robert Demachy, and the Hofmeisters. Newcomers included Imogen Cunningham and Paul Strand. The exhibition of 82 photographs was impressive enough to warrant a *New York Times* review and to elicit Stieglitz's scorn.[61] At the end of the year, Ehrich sponsored another exhibition organized by White's group, this time of "old master" photographs, including works by D. O. Hill and Julia Margaret Cameron. Arranged by Coburn, the exhibition traveled to Buffalo's Albright Art Gallery. Coburn made all the prints in the exhibition, printing from the original paper negatives of Hill and Thomas Keith and making copy negatives from original prints by Cameron and Lewis Carroll. The exhibition was on view in Buffalo from 30 January to 28 February 1915. In his introductory comments, Coburn wrote: "When we become acquainted with the work of Clarence White and the little group of earnest friends who have gathered about him, we realize that Hill, Keith, Cameron, and Carroll did not do their pioneer work in vain, for photography now is at last coming into its own, respected for the things it will do within its limitations." Ironically, Coburn identified the trend toward straight photography—"respected for the things it will do within its limitations"—with White rather than Stieglitz and Strand (Buffalo Fine Arts Academy brochure, New York Public Library).

The following year, Ehrich offered White his Print Gallery, also at 707 Fifth Avenue, for a group exhibition juried by Henry W. Kent, secretary of the Metropolitan Museum of Art; Frank Weitenkampf, print curator at the New York Public Library; and Albert Sterner, a portrait painter and illustrator whom White had long admired. Also in 1915, White, Coburn, Dickson, and Struss worked with the Photographic Society of Philadelphia to mount an exhibition at the Rosenbach Galleries, owned by the prominent bibliophile Dr. A. S. W. Rosenbach. Making a conscious effort to avoid "cliques or schools," the group again tried unsuccessfully to solicit work from Stieglitz despite his adversarial history with the Philadelphia Society.[62]

LAURA GILPIN

Bryce Canyon, Utah, Fall 1930

White's group exhibition efforts culminated in the formation of the Pictorial Photographers of America (PPA) in January 1916.[63] In Struss's words, he, White, and Dickson were "the three conspirators" behind the idea for a national organization, which grew out of the local exhibitions and the publication of *Platinum Print*.[64] White was the organization's president and Dickson its secretary—titles that confirmed the relationship between the two men during the *Platinum Print* years. In October 1916 the PPA's inaugural exhibition was held under the auspices of the American Institute of Graphic Arts (AIGA) at the National Arts Club, where the inaugural exhibition of the Photo-Secession had taken place in 1902. The choice of venue, however, had more to do with Goudy's influence on White than with a desire for historical resonance.

Goudy was a founding member of the AIGA, an organization formed in 1914 to "aid and encourage all those engaged in graphic arts in America to form a cooperative center for interchange of ideas and information to stimulate public interest and appreciation and as far as possible to create a desire for better products, by publication of literature and designs, by exhibitions, [and] by educational lectures . . . (*Exhibition of American Printing*, National Arts Club, 28 March–14 April 1916)." The AIGA was a model for the PPA, which aimed at reforming public taste as much as advancing the art of photography.[65] Both organizations held regular meetings and exhibitions at the National Arts Club, which invited various arts and crafts groups to use its facilities.

Even the content of the 1916 exhibition showed the AIGA's influence. In addition to 245 prints by pictorial photographers, the exhibition included a historical and scientific section representing processes from daguerreotypes to X-rays, an extensive installation on color, and a variety of photographic illustrations. This approach to photographic history departed from the pictorial norm, which had featured "masters" of the medium. It resembled the AIGA's exhibitions, which surveyed the evolution of techniques and forms during the 500-year history of printing arts. The relationship between White and the AIGA was reciprocal, for White became a regular member of its exhibition committee, beginning with the spring show of 1916.[66]

In a 1919 AIGA catalogue, White summarized his belief in the usefulness of uniting printing and photography:

> No more fitting association for exhibiting photography can be suggested than with printing, process-printing, advertising and posters. . . . Let the plate engraver study the photographs together with the various processes and their effects. Let the photographer also study the reproductive processes and the various results obtained with different screens, inks, and papers. Through such a procedure . . . a closer relationship and understanding [will be] established between the artist, the plate engraver, and the public in general.[67]

ANNE W. BRIGMAN
Invictus, 1925

Although the PPA eschewed the exclusivity of the Photo-Secession, it did not enlist the nation's local camera clubs, which it scorned.[68] The PPA saw itself as the rightful heir of the Photo-Secession, but with a difference. It wished to avoid Stieglitz's destructive political intrigues and to use pictorial photography as a tool of art education. The PPA's first initiative was to circulate two exhibitions to sixteen art museums, libraries, and art associations throughout the east and midwest.[69] A traveling lecture series was discussed though never executed. In 1917 the PPA issued its first annual report, which replaced *Photo=Graphic Art* as the White group publication. In less than five years, a small band of "conspirators" meeting in a bookshop had developed an institutional identity.

During these same years, White established the Clarence H. White School of Photography in downtown Manhattan. Moving from his Fifth Avenue studio and Morningside Heights apartment, White opened the school in 1914 in a brownstone at 230 East 11th Street. It was a family business, with classrooms and darkroom on the lower floors, the White residence on the upper floor, and Jane White as household manager and school administrator. The school's advisory board consisted of close friends, including Käsebier, Day, Coburn, Struss, and Scott. In this intimate environment, students became members of the Whites' extended family.[70]

The school was located on the edge of Greenwich Village in a building adjoining St. Mark's-in-the-Bouwerie, New York's second oldest church. White's landlord, the Reverend William Norman Guthrie, was concerned less with his traditional Episcopalian parishioners than with the neighborhood's bohemian residents, whom he lured to his congregation with a nonsectarian theology that celebrated the liberation of body and soul through dance. The church regularly hosted performances of European folk, Native American, and modern dance. Although Jane White complained that Reverend Guthrie was remiss with repairs, he was appointed an advisor to the school and lectured on "the relationship between photography and art."[71]

Like Reverend Guthrie, White was a modern dance enthusiast and illustrated an invitation to one of Guthrie's dance recitals. White planned but never completed a book of modern dance photographs, which Goudy offered to publish.[72] White's enthusiasm for modern dance was shared by his students, who were more productive. An issue of *Platinum Print* was devoted to dance in 1915; in 1917 Struss completed *The Female Figure*, a portfolio of twenty nudes in modern dance poses; and in 1921 Dickson published *Poems of the Dance*, an anthology of poems illustrated with his own photographs.

Although America's entry into World War I decreased the school's enrollment, White found the 11th Street house too small and in 1917 moved to larger quarters at 122 East 17th Street, on the corner of Irving Place. Again White chose a location rich

AMY WHITTEMORE

Poplars at Night, ca. 1910

in historical and artistic associations. Known as the Washington Irving House, this large residence was thought to have been built in the 1840s for the author of *The Legend of Sleepy Hollow*. From the early 1890s until 1911, it was home to actress Elsie de Wolfe and literary agent Elisabeth Marbury, a couple whose inventive decor and dazzling guest register brought fame to the address.[73] The house was conveniently located two blocks from the Studio Building of the National Arts Club at 119 East 19th Street, where the PPA held its meetings.

As a photographer, White was an unskilled technician who "was lost if you deprived him of Orthonon plates, Rodinal developer and platinum paper."[74] To compensate for his deficiency, White hired Paul L. Anderson, an electrical engineer and close friend of Struss, to teach technique at the school.[75] Although White preferred straight platinum printing to elaborate darkroom manipulation, he encouraged Anderson to teach the full range of pictorial processes, an approach consistent with White's pedagogic flexibility.

In hiring Anderson in 1914, White showed unusual open-mindedness, for Anderson was an outspoken advocate of aesthetic views that were contrary to White's own. In the year Anderson began teaching at the school, he published his first book, *Pictorial Landscape-Photography*, which dismissed Dow's theory of composition that justified the expressive potential of abstract form in favor of the competing theory of Henry Rankin Poore, a conservative professor at the Pennsylvania Academy of the Fine Arts.[76] In 1917 Anderson published his White School lectures as *Pictorial Photography: Its Principles and Practice*, which gave technical advice but also attacked the unconventional conduct of the avant-garde artist.[77]

If Anderson was straitlaced and artistically conservative, Max Weber, whom White enlisted to teach art appreciation and design, was the opposite. An Eastern European Jewish immigrant who spoke English with an accent, Weber spent five years in Paris absorbing the art of Cézanne, Matisse, and Picasso. When he returned to New York in 1909, he was America's most avant-garde painter and found the city a desolate "north pole of art."[78] Joining Stieglitz's circle, Weber was Stieglitz's mentor in modern art until their break in early 1911. White offered Weber spiritual and financial support until 1918, when Weber left the school.

Weber was not without training and experience as a teacher. Before Paris he studied with Dow in the teachers' program at Pratt Institute and taught art in the midwest. Although Weber's art was more advanced than Dow's, he remained loyal to Dow, and in later years, declared: "When you ask me who was my greatest teacher, it was Dow." Weber delivered a talk to White's students at Teachers College in 1910, and soon after White opened his summer school, he asked Weber to teach there.[79]

participant in Weber's critiques at the Little Book-shop, Strand may have benefited from Weber's thinking, which derived from the same sources as those discussed at 291.[89] Seen in context, Strand's abstractions, each of which bore the title *Photograph* (fig. 4), were masterful but not unique.

As Laura Gilpin noted in her article, "The Need for Design in Photography," abstract still life became the foundation for teaching design at the White School:

BERNARD S. HORNE
"Design," Photo=Graphic Art, *vol. 3, no. 2*

> How can we acquire this knowledge and skill [of design]? By careful study of still life for one thing. Making arrangements of objects of all sorts and descriptions, experimenting with all kinds of lighting, setting ourselves definite problems to solve. These are the five finger exercises and scales of composition.[90]

While still life offered a controlled encounter with composition, many students chose to leave the studio to explore the skewed perspectives and bewildering geometries of the city's streets. Struss was the pioneer of this approach, making cubist-inspired cityscapes as early as 1911, well before Weber's classes. Arthur Chapman's series on Greenwich Village resulted directly from Weber's teaching. Avoiding the Village's tourist traps, Chapman sought anonymous subjects "with neither signboards nor names."[91] His tour de force was *Diagonals* (page 69), which was chosen by Coburn for the 1915 RPS exhibition and published in *Platinum Print* (vol. 2, no. 1). It portrays a view down Christopher Street obscured by a tangle of intersecting planes formed by the snow-covered El station, where Chapman stood. As Chapman explained:

> I used one of the Sixth Avenue elevated stations twice a day for several months and then found "Diagonals." . . . I have been discovering for myself that pictures can be "seen" anywhere, if only the artist will forget that he is looking at familiar things.[92]

Chapman's work, like that of many of White's students, combined abstract composition with soft focus and platinum printing.

In keeping with White's teachings, Chapman published a booklet of eight of his Greenwich Village photographs in 1915. Dickson, in his introduction to the booklet, noted Chapman's "fine adjustment of his needs to design and the decoration of space." The booklet advertised the sale of Chapman's photographs and may have tempted him to turn professional. Chapman nevertheless kept his union job as a typographer for nearly fifty years.[93]

White himself was also influenced by Weber's teaching. Asked during an interview in 1918 about the effect of "cubistic art" on pictorial photography, White replied:

Yes, it has gotten into photography to a slight extent, but I am loth to call it cubism or any similar ism. The development of modern art, I think, is in the direction of construction; and construction, picture construction, applies to photography as definitely as it applies to painting and other art. Indeed, a great feeling of the need for this has expressed itself in connection with photography.[94]

(figure 4)

PAUL STRAND
"Photograph (Porch Shadows),"
Camera Work 49–50 *(June 1917)*

During the teens, White's work literally moved "in the direction of construction," as shown in his photographs of 1917 of ship construction in Bath, Maine. These ships that White observed were headed for war. As a socialist, White was anti-war; and as a father of a son in the army, he was fearful. White avoided the political content of his subject—his studies of the criss-crossed scaffolding of half-finished hulks sacrifice literal representation for abstract form. Another abstract composition, which White used for an exhibition announcement in 1923, is his only known photograph of the urban scene (fig. 5). In the raking midday sun, White photographed a row of street-cleaning wagons under one of the huge piers of Manhattan Bridge. The wagons' shapes and shadows form a repetitive geometrical pattern under the arching shadow of the bridge's steel structure.

More important to White than modern art, however, was open-mindedness. As he observed in the same interview of 1918:

Let [the photographer] leave the mind open and that will tell him what to express. . . . He should be moved by his subject. If he is not, he will become blind to the most beautiful aspects of nature. That is the interesting thing of nature. . . . The light is continually changing, and [the photographer] has combinations and variations that a man with a preconceived idea will miss, and in photography that is the most impressive thing—that it can record those subtleties.[95]

White sought originality in every style, from the manipulated gum print to the abstract cityscape.

A conservative student whose individual vision White enthusiastically endorsed was Antoinette Hervey, who documented the construction of the Episcopal Church of St. John the Divine over a thirty-year period. Her luminous platinum prints of the cathedral (page 71) recall those of the English pictorial photographer Frederick Evans. The wife of the former president of Columbia Teachers College,[96] Hervey was an ama-

ARTHUR D. CHAPMAN

Diagonals (Christopher Street from the
8th Street station of the Sixth Avenue
El, New York), 1913

teur who nonetheless fulfilled White's ideals for socially productive art photography. She lectured on "careers in photography for women" and illustrated *The Word in Stone*, a beautifully printed fund-raising brochure for the cathedral.[97]

Hervey, however, was not the typical White student. Most came to New York for "training in the vocation of photography,"[98] took White's thirty-week course, and returned home to set up a portrait studio and solicit illustration assignments.[99] White himself provided the model for this career, even though most of his energy went into teaching. The courses that he added to the school's basic curriculum reveal his intent to bridge the gap between pictorial and professional photography. In 1919 White and Goudy began teaching "Printing and Photography Related," directed at "the cultivation of taste and the use of printing as an artistic craft" in books, magazines, and advertising; and a remedial course was added for the professional photographer "to call forth a greater exercise of his art-sense in the service of portraits by photography."[100]

Among those who fulfilled White's ideal of the professional art photographer were Clara Sipprell, Laura Gilpin, and Doris Ulmann.[101] Throughout their careers, these women specialized in portraiture and commercial illustration and participated in pictorial exhibitions. Their interest in folk cultures—Sipprell's studies of peasant life in Yugoslavia and Mexico, Gilpin's of Native Americans, and Ulmann's of African Americans in the South and Appalachian culture—place them within the arts and crafts tradition, which valued non-Western handicraft. Gilpin and Ulmann published their photographs not only in magazines but in high-quality photographically illustrated books.

(figure 5)

White's appeal to women students has been attributed to his gentle manner, not always in flattering terms. In an interview, Ralph Steiner recalled: ". . . I think the very fact that he didn't press hard for absolute perfection, but always found something to praise, won him the worship of a lot of ladies."[102] A more likely explanation is that White took women seriously, an attitude fostered by his arts and crafts heritage. According to Gilpin, Stieglitz and Steichen "were not the least bit interested in women photographers."[103] White accepted them into his school without bias, and several women students—including Gilpin and Sipprell—established supportive relationships with Käsebier, who was at the top of the field as an art professional. It was more than

ANTOINETTE B. HERVEY

*Base of a Great Column (in the
nave of the Cathedral of St. John the
Divine, New York), 1929*

FRANCES SPALDING

Columns, Low Memorial Library,
Columbia University, New York, 1922

BERNARD S. HORNE

Design—Princeton, ca. 1917

White's personal qualities, however, that drew women to his school. During the years before World War I, American women entered the work force in unprecedented numbers and adopted the lifestyle of the independent "new woman."[104] The teaching profession, which was traditionally open to women, was rapidly expanding, and White was affiliated with teacher training programs at Columbia and the Brooklyn Institute.[105] Moreover, photography did not demand the rigid courses of study and apprenticeships required of the older arts, which were often unavailable to women.

An added attraction for women photographers was White's expertise in home portraiture, a new specialty in which sitters were photographed in their own homes.[106] Home portraiture was a natural outgrowth of White's artistic photography, which had centered on his own family. Women, White believed, were "particularly qualified for this branch of work, in that they can more easily become a part of the family and can study the conditions of the family life more closely."[107]

In the essay "Photography as a Profession for Women," White encouraged women to attend a school "where one gets the fundamentals which are practically the same for all branches of photography—the understanding of the chemical and physical reactions involved in the many processes which are being used and developed; the cultivation of a sense of the beautiful, an aptitude for composition and design, which no photographic school should fail to teach."[108] No doubt the school that White had in mind was his own, which by 1920 had matured from an informal summer workshop into an established New York institution.

A VISION FULFILLED: 1920–1925

During the early 1920s White's organizational program took its final form. The school moved to larger quarters and the Art Center became the home of the PPA. Together, these institutions offered the fledgling photographer technical training, art education, and career opportunities.

In 1920, the lease on the Washington Irving House expired, and White moved to 460 West 144th Street in northern Manhattan.[109] Approaching fifty, White was still living from hand to mouth and at the mercy of his landlord. This time, instead of renting, he formed the Clarence H. White Realty Corporation and borrowed $25,000 to buy and renovate a four-story Victorian brownstone in Hamilton Heights, a pleasant residential neighborhood in Harlem, just north of City College. The new location was convenient to Teachers College but a long commute to Brooklyn, and in 1922, White resigned from the Brooklyn Institute faculty.

The new site brought increased darkroom and studio space, and room for equipment for a new course in nonphotographic printmaking techniques. The house, however, required an aesthetic makeover. Its "Queen Anne cornices . . . 'beautiful' wall paper, and a rich cherry finish at war with any conceivable color scheme" were hopelessly bourgeois. With the help of students, friends, and alumni, White stripped away the ornament, painted the walls "harmonious tints of pearl gray," hung them "with an Oriental print or two," and draped the mantel with "some simple stuff from India."[110] White's first lesson to his students was that art begins with one's everyday surroundings. Their photographs of the school's rooms show that the lesson was well learned.

In forming a corporation, White shared the era's faith in venture capitalism, but his monetary goals were modest. His shareholders were friends and alumni who held the school's mortgage, and it was hoped that when the mortgage was paid off, the corporation would dissolve and White would own the building. Despite the financial guidance of Charles H. Jaeger and Walter Hervey—husbands of Doris Ulmann and Antoinette Hervey—and the fund-raising efforts of wealthy alumni like Bernard Horne, the school teetered on the brink of financial failure. White's ability to pay off the mortgage was based on a projected enrollment of fifty students a year, but White insisted on retaining his small classes of fifteen. In 1922 White tried to pay off the year's debt by producing twenty portfolios of his own prints for $300 each.[111] Rumors of the school's closing reached F. R. Fraprie, the editor of *American Photography*, who, in a rueful condolence note to White, remarked that the school "was too good to succeed."[112] The rumors proved premature, and the school managed to survive numerous financial crises.

Stieglitz once remarked that White "could never earn real money,"[113] and it seems he never tried. According to Jane White, "finances were not a consideration with Clarence—& what he felt was best for his school he went right ahead & did . . . with always the optimistic feeling that the future was his & he would be able to clear everything up."[114] White put his students' needs before his own: he limited yearly enrollment to guarantee his effectiveness as a teacher and to assure his students ample darkroom use; he offered evening and part-time classes to accommodate students who held daytime jobs; and he even tried a summer session in the city for students who could not afford the stay in Connecticut. Not surprisingly, White displayed rare public anger when an editorial described all photography schools as "commercial":

> In view of the fact that I am the director of a School of Photography, we are not a commercial institution, even though I feel that we have the privilege of making a living by it, which we do not. . . . [O]ur standard has always been to plant the "seed of enthusiasm" above any thought of profit in our School. Our record is behind us, and we would be very glad, indeed, to have you investigate it.[115]

ALLIE BRAMBERG BODE

San Francisco Xavier, Seminario de
San Martín, Tepotzotlán, Mexico, 1925

LOUISE HALSEY

North Gate, Columbia University, and
Main and Household Arts Buildings,
Teachers College, New York, ca. 1911

IRA W. MARTIN

At the Plaza, New York, ca. 1930

HENRY W. SHEPARD

Angles, from the Window of the
Clarence H. White School of
Photography, 460 W. 144th Street,
New York (The Morning Sun),
1924/1925

IRA W. MARTIN

Clapboard House with Shadows, by 1934

DORIS ULMANN

Abstraction (Metropolitan
Museum of Art Seen Through
the Greywacke Arch, Central
Park, New York), 1917

FRANCESCA S. BOSTWICK

Bruges, Belgium, ca. 1910

Modernist magazine photography extended beyond the lecture series onto the pages of Condé Nast's *Vanity Fair*. In 1921 and 1922 the magazine published a series of full-page features on modern photography, including Charles Sheeler's "cubist architecture," Man Ray's photograms, and Francis Bruguière's light abstractions. White's relationship with Campbell no doubt explains the inclusion of White students Ira Martin, Paul Outerbridge Jr., and Margaret Watkins in the series.[120] Watkins's *Vanity Fair* feature, "Photography Comes into the Kitchen," displayed a group of still-life design exercises that transformed household utensils into elegant, space-filling compositions (fig. 6). Her subtle manipulation of value, texture, and form recalls the delicate tonal harmonies of White's own work. More than any other student, Watkins, who taught technique in the school during the 1920s and was secretary of the PPA, carried White's sensibility into the modern era.

Photography Comes into the Kitchen
A Group of Photographs by Margaret Watkins Showing Modernist, or Cubist, Patterns in Composition

(figure 6)

MARGARET WATKINS
"Photography Comes into the Kitchen," Vanity Fair, *vol. 17, no. 8 (October 1921): 60.*

As the White School flourished, so did the Art Center, which White helped to establish to advance the industrial, craft, and graphic arts. The lifetime goal of art philanthropist Helen Sargent Hitchcock,[121] the center provided a home for seven arts organizations: the Society of Illustrators (founded 1901), the New York Society of Craftsmen (1906), the Stowaways (1907), the Art Alliance (1914), the American Institute of Graphic Arts (1914), the Pictorial Photographers of America (1917), and the Art Directors Club (1920).[122] In 1920 Hitchcock succeeded in raising $140,000 to purchase and renovate elegant twin townhouses at 65–67 East 56th Street in midtown Manhattan. In October of 1921 the center opened with an impressive array of patrician art patrons from its board of directors and advisory committee in attendance. White was a member of the board, and in 1922 he started the *Art Center Bulletin*.[123]

The Art Center revitalized the arts and crafts movement in New York and replaced the National Arts Club as a "clearing house" for arts and crafts organizations.[124] Indeed, its three most active member organizations—the AIGA, the PPA, and the ADC—met and exhibited at the Arts Club until the Art Center opened. Casting off nineteenth-century suspicions of machine-made products and business interests, the center promoted "art and industry" by establishing a noncommercial environment in which artists, designers, and entrepreneurs could mingle.

With White as president until 1922, the PPA was especially active at the new center. There, it held monthly one-person exhibitions, lectures, and print competitions,

WYNN RICHARDS

Still Life—Candlestick, Flowers in a
Vase, Books, and Scissors, ca. 1918

and, beginning in 1920, published lavish annuals with short essays and well-reproduced prints. The PPA discontinued its schedule of traveling exhibitions, replacing it in 1923 with a biennial international salon as ambitious as the well-established Pittsburgh salon.

For the PPA, the presence of the Art Directors Club at the Art Center proved edifying. Art direction developed as a profession in the teens in response to the growth of illustrated magazines and advertising into national industries. Supervising the choice and disposition of magazine illustrations, art directors mediated between two ill-matched constituencies: artists, who accepted the lure of advertising assignments with trepidation, and advertisers, who viewed the effect of art on sales with skepticism.[125] "What is needed," wrote proselytizer Earnest Elmo Calkins, "is a less stiff and condescending state of mind on the part of the world's greatest artists [and] a less intolerant and narrow-minded attitude on the part of the world's greatest advertisers."[126] The rationale for quality art in advertising, he argued, was not only increased sales but elevated public taste.

In the early 1920s art directors fiercely debated the appropriateness of modern art in advertising—whether modern art was a cultural aberration or "the spirit of the times." In the PPA annual of 1922, Heyworth Campbell, the Art Directors Club's first president, derided the "work of youngsters" under the sway of modernism as symptomatic of cultural malaise and an "urge to be different, different merely for the sake of being different."[127] Two years later he shifted sides in the debate, embracing modern art as a formal language that could serve varied ends, including advertising:

> Art is not a thing to be done, but the best way of doing that which is necessary to be done. This brings a tobacco advertisement into the realm of art as truly as the designing of a cathedral.[128]

The watershed in the popular acceptance of modern art was the Exposition des Arts Décoratifs in Paris, which in 1925 heralded modern design in utilitarian objects, from fashion and furniture to architecture and advertising. The *Art Center Bulletin* declared that the exposition was "the great international convention of twentieth-century artistic ideals. It existed to dedicate a new style; it marked the passing of the old order."[129]

The unnaturalistic color and complex geometries of futurism and cubism appeared briefly in advertising in the mid-1920s, but these experiments were quickly rejected as affected and confusing (fig. 7).[130] The most successful adaptation of modern art to advertising was in product display. Instead of relying on copy and story-telling illustrations to present a sales pitch, the art director conveyed his message more simply and effectively by showing the product in an eye-catching way, arrestingly cropped or from an unusual viewpoint.

White School photographers pioneered this approach several years before painters adopted it. Many of White's best students were among the first advertising photographers, including Margaret Bourke-White (who was enrolled with White at Teachers College), Outerbridge, Steiner, Watkins, Wynn Richards, Ira Martin, and Anton Bruehl. Outerbridge's Ide Shirt Company advertisement, which appeared in *Vanity Fair* in November 1922, best demonstrates the new style (fig. 8). A sculptural white collar seen against a grid of black-and-white paper squares seems to hover over a gargantuan chessboard or a Lilliputian linoleum floor. The sharp focus makes legible the trade name inside the collar, as well as the neck size, 14 ³/₄, of the slim imaginary owner. Outerbridge's visual wit transformed straightforward product display into an image more compelling than the Ide Company's routine advertisements, which featured a photograph of the dapper customer himself (fig. 9).

In the 1925 essay "The Use of Photography in Advertising," published in the *Art Center Bulletin*, Temple Scott championed the White School's still life for product advertising.[131] "If the photographer is an artist," Scott wrote, photography can "set forth arrestingly the value or the utility of the commodity." More tasteful and truthful than the writer's shrill copy or the painter's prettified imagery was the "implied opinion" of "presenting the article itself to the best advantage." Scott offered numerous examples from White and his students: an illustration from White's 1912 Barnard calendar; still-life exercises by Bernard Horne, Outerbridge, and Steiner; and a J. Walter Thompson advertisement by Watkins.

(figure 7)

SERGEI SOUDEÏKINE
Le Sacre du Printemps, in "Steinway, the Instrument of the Immortals," Vogue, vol. 73, no. 3 (2 February 1929): 129.

Two pairs of images show the shifting relationship between painting and photography in the new advertising. Before World War I, pictorial photographs were rarely used for advertisements, and when they were, they imitated the style of popular illustration. In a 1916 advertisement, Karl Struss photographed a business executive in distress ("I was nervously bankrupt—my last scintilla of nerve force expended!"), who required the pacifying benefit of Sanatogen, "the food-tonic approved by science" (fig. 10). Struss's genre scene makes no sense without the copywriter's narrative, and his soft-focus style was clearly based upon an illustrator's precedent (fig. 11).

By the late 1920s modernist product display was common coin in advertising, and photography set the example. In 1929 the Art Directors Club awarded two medals to the Oxford Paper Company, one for a colored drawing by Joseph Sinel (fig. 12) and the other for a photograph by Ralph Steiner (page 109). Printed on Oxford paper, the advertisements serve as product samples: the wash drawing of pots containing the three primary colors shows how well the paper receives color; the photograph of type-writer keys shows how it receives halftone reproduction. The two images are similarly composed: closeups of circular objects seen from an overhead oblique viewpoint. The photograph, with its interplay of large simple forms and subtle tonal gradations, is the more visually compelling of the images; a White School design exercise from 1921, it preceded the drawing by eight years and was almost certainly its model.

(figure 8)

PAUL OUTERBRIDGE JR.
"Ide Collars," Vanity Fair, *vol. 19,
no. 3 (November 1922): 5.*

Although photography was still confined to black and white, its presumption of "truth" was a powerful lure for art directors, offering them "realism with just that touch of idealism."[132] In his introduction to the 1924 ADC annual, Gordon Aymar, an art director for J. Walter Thompson, appropriated the language of straight photography to define this approach:

Good composition and the proper selection of material, photographed in a direct and honest way, are very evident. The place of the photograph in advertising is unquestioned. It can accomplish things which no drawing or painting can possibly do. On the other hand, forced beyond the limits of its own inherent characteristics, it becomes false and loses that sense of reality which is its chief asset.[133]

To the dismay of Stieglitz and Strand, straight photography, like modern art, had mutated from an avant-garde ideology into an advertising technique.

In July 1925, as his hope for a new commercial photography was being realized, White died in Mexico City of a heart attack. The 1926 PPA annual was dedicated to his memory. It included a section on advertising photography with an introduction by Margaret Watkins, who spoke for the new generation that White had nurtured:

[I]n the days of the Photo-Secession . . . no devout pictorialist would have deigned to descend to advertising. In their desire to establish photography as an art they became a bit precious; crudeness was distressing, materialism shunned.

With Cézanne, Matisse, Picasso came a new approach. Soulfulness was taboo, romance derided, anecdote scorned; beauty of subject was superseded by beauty of design, and the relation of ideas gave place to the relation of forms. . . . The comprehending photographer saw, paused, and seized his camera! And while the more conservative workers still exhibited photographs beautiful in the accepted sense, strange offerings startled the juries. . . . But the eye of the advertiser was alert. Here were possibilities. . . .[134]

(figure 9)

ARTIST UNKNOWN
"Kentstreet, Ide Streetline Shirts," Vanity Fair, *vol. 18, no. 3 (May 1922): 11.*

CARRYING ON WITHOUT WHITE: 1925–1942

When White died, Stieglitz asserted that "the school that [White] founded will not be able to exist without him. He was the school."[135] Stieglitz's fatalistic pronouncement proved untrue, for Jane White took over as director and the school remained open until 1942. The loss of its spiritual leader, however, threw the school into crisis. Fearful of losing its investment, the Clarence H. White Realty Corporation placed conditions upon Mrs. White's residency, offering her a three-year lease.[136] A motion picture course that White had planned for the 1926 season was canceled. A dispute erupted between Mrs. White and the alumni association concerning its plan to produce a memorial volume of White's photographs without her consent; the book never materialized, and the association languished.[137] And Margaret Watkins, who had been fervently loyal to White, threatened to sue Mrs. White for money owed her.[138] To help make ends meet, the Canaan property was sold, and, with the help of Laura Gilpin, a selection of White's prints was sold to the Library of Congress.[139]

Through sheer force of will and hard work, Jane White kept the school on an even keel. To increase income, enrollment steadily grew, from 20 students in 1922 to 106 in 1939. The faculty for the art appreciation course was replenished with Teachers College graduates, and White School graduates were enlisted to teach the technical course. The Whites' eldest son, Lewis, a printer, followed in Goudy's footsteps by designing White School publications and serving on the cooperative teaching staff. Bruehl, Outerbridge, and Steiner, who were among the school's most distinguished alumni, served on its advisory board, and Bruehl and Outerbridge taught occasional courses. Steichen, whose work

ARTHUR D. CHAPMAN
Max Weber, 1914

for Condé Nast and J. Walter Thompson made him the premier magazine photographer of the day, regularly lectured to the students. Led by these teachers, the school continued to train successful magazine photographers, such as Sara Parsons, an advertising specialist, and Emelie Danielson, who became a staff photographer for *House Beautiful*.

In its later years, the school's successful graduates established solid but unspectacular careers in commercial photography. A survey of the school's archives shows that by the mid-1930s the quality and originality of student work had substantially declined. Still life and architecture, both of which require a solid sense of composition, were the students' strong suits, but these became increasingly formulaic. Manipulative printing processes were abandoned in favor of straight printing, and a dye transfer color course was added. Portraiture, fashion, and narrative advertising remained undeveloped, but in 1940 *Life* photographer Eliot Elisofon began teaching a course in photojournalism.

The loss of creativity at the school was due largely to the loss of White, but changes in the advertising industry and the economy also played a part. In the early 1920s White's students entered a small and unformed field. Art directors were still uncertain of what photography could accomplish and allowed photographers to complete their assignments with little interference after discussion of the marketing concept. Many in the advertising business claimed that advertising could provide art education for the general public. Encouraged by the economy's dizzying rate of growth, artistic pronouncements sometimes ran to hyperbole: Stanley Resor, president of J. Walter Thompson, claimed that advertising and the skyscraper were America's contribution to art history, and Steichen often compared his task to Michelangelo's.[140]

(figure 10)

KARL STRUSS
"Sanatogen," The Outlook, *vol. 113, no. 13 (28 March 1917): 561.*

The Depression collapsed these grandiose expectations and constrained artistic freedom. Fearing for their jobs, art directors were loath to challenge the injunctions of advertisers, and the advice of pollsters and behavioral psychologists became more compelling than the rhetoric of art. Reined in from above, art directors exerted tighter control on those below. Bruehl recalled that in the mid-1920s, "art directors were often fine artists in their own right" and gave him "a pretty free hand." "Later on," he complained, "it became much more cut and dried. The agency would come in with a complete layout and you had to pretty much stick to it. That's when the fun went out of things."[141]

Although Hollywood movies, tabloid journalism, and comic strips dominated advertising imagery in the thirties, modernism remained a photographic style that was well suited to the era's streamlined objects and architecture. White School students were ably trained for an uncontroversial specialty within an increasingly impersonal profession. Student expectations also changed; in a depressed economy, they sought job training, not artistic refinement.[142]

Despite these limitations, the White School easily surpassed its two principal competitors—the New York Institute of Photography and the Studio School of Art Photography. The New York Institute, established in 1910, was a strictly commercial school without artistic ambition.[143] Open all year, it offered no organized program and extracted fees in exchange for hours of individualized instruction. The Studio School, which opened in 1920, offered small classes by Benjamin Rabinovitch, a portrait photographer who practiced an unrepentant pictorialism well into the 1930s. By contrast, the White School was state accredited[144] and successfully balanced artistic and technical training. It is not surprising that in 1938 Steichen advised a would-be photographer that she should attend "an excellent school in New York called the Clarence White School."[145]

In its final years, the school was directed by the Whites' third son, Clarence Jr., who was born shortly after White moved to New York, and was eighteen years old when his father died. A graduate of the program in 1927, Clarence Jr. was a skilled technician without artistic talent. He became an instructor in 1931 and in 1937 he took over as director when his mother retired, administering the school conscientiously, family-style.[146] In 1940 Clarence Jr. moved the school to a large elegant townhouse at 32 West 74th Street, where he reinstituted an ambitious lecture program and revived the alumni association and its bulletin.[147] Among the lecturers were Max Weber, Bruehl, and Steichen; younger photographers Barbara Morgan, Gjon Mili, and George Platt Lynes; and prominent authorities Beaumont Newhall of The Museum of Modern Art, Roy Stryker of the Farm Security Administration, and Dr. M. F. Agha, Heyworth Campbell's successor at Condé Nast. Films such as Strand's *The Wave* were shown, and exhibitions included Barbara Morgan's dance photographs and photographs of the FSA. Poorly timed with the mobilization for World War II, the move proved too costly, and White resorted to giving his

(figure 11)

ARTIST UNKNOWN
"Sanatogen," Vogue, *vol. 45, no. 3 (1 February 1915): 87.*

father's prints to staff members to pay their salaries.[148] When the school failed to attract government support to train military photographers, it went bankrupt in 1942, twenty-eight years after its founding.

The school survived the Art Center, which had depended on the largesse of wealthy philanthropists in the 1920s and had fallen victim to the Depression in 1933. At White's death in 1925, however, the Art Center was flush with success. The popular embrace of modern design in the wake of the Paris exposition of 1925 affirmed the center's mission, and the exhibition of avant-garde paintings from the estate of John Quinn, a prominent lawyer, drew huge crowds and extensive newspaper coverage. John D. Rockefeller funded a three-year director's appointment, which was given to Dow-trained art professor Alon Bement. With plans to expand its annual expenditures by sixty percent, the center embarked on an ambitious $700,000 endowment campaign. Art director Earnest Elmo Calkins foresaw a bright future:

It is the night of May 20, 1950, the night of the great art event of the year—the spring exhibition at the new Art Center, covering two city blocks on West Fifty-seventh Street, overlooking the North River.[149]

In the late 1920s, the center launched many forward-looking initiatives: a campaign to improve the design of wayside roadstands, an "opportunity gallery" for monthly one-person exhibitions by emerging artists, an annual exhibition by African American artists, and a ground-breaking exhibition of foreign advertising and industrial photography.[150] Despite these efforts, the center raised only $100,000 toward its endowment and continued to survive on a few large individual gifts. In 1929, it merged with the New York Regional Art Council, which was founded two years earlier with a grant from the Carnegie Foundation.[151] When the economy hit its nadir in 1932, the center and the Regional Art Council were dissolved.[152]

While the Art Center remained open, the PPA thrived. In addition to monthly lectures, exhibitions, and print competitions, it sponsored its third international salon in 1929 and produced a fifth annual. Perhaps because of the high quality of the annual, Margaret Bourke-White, Nicholas Haz, Lewis Hine, and Karl Struss, who had broken with the PPA ten years before, were among its new members that year. The PPA's president from 1927 to

(figure 12)

JOSEPH SINEL
"*Oxford Paper Company,*" Art Directors
Annual, *vol. 8 (1929): 8.*

JOSEPH SINEL—OXFORD PAPERS
Oxford Paper Co.
W. L. Brann, Inc.
MEDAL

RALPH STEINER

Typewriter Keys, 1921

1937 was Ira Martin, a White graduate and chief photographer for the Frick Art Reference Library. Shortly after becoming president, Martin initiated a new PPA bulletin, *Light and Shade*,[153] and enlisted architectural photographer Thurman Rotan as its editor; the bulletin proselytized for the "modern school" of straight photography; it reviewed exhibitions at Alma Reed's Delphic Studios, Julien Levy's gallery, and Stieglitz's American Place, and featured works by industrial and advertising photographers (fig. 13).

As the New York-based leader of a national organization, Martin tried to educate a provincial audience without alienating it. His sponsorship of modernism, straight photography, and commercial photography was at odds, however, with trends outside New York. A review in *Light and Shade* (June 1931, p. 4) of Edward Weston's 1931 exhibition at Delphic Studios reveals Martin's diffidence:

Anton Bruehl

"FOR THE PROMOTION OF PHOTOGRAPHY AS AN ART"
OCTOBER 1929. PUBLISHED MONTHLY BY PICTORIAL
PHOTOGRAPHERS OF AMERICA, 65 EAST 56 STREET, N. Y.

(figure 13)

ANTON BRUEHL
Light and Shade, *vol. 2, no. 1*
(October 1929): cover

[V]olumes have been printed and thousands of reproductions have been made of the so called "old school" photography but the "modern," or work of the moment, necessarily cannot be universally seen or presented up to date. If we seem, therefore, to favor this type, it is only because we feel that workers throughout the country would like to keep posted on the new efforts of experimental workers and not that we are promoting any particular styles of photography.

After the closing of the Art Center in 1933, the PPA waned, becoming increasingly self-absorbed and indistinguishable from the nation's local camera clubs.[154] In 1937 Martin gave up the PPA presidency to reactivate the international salon, which had languished since 1929. His efforts to bridge the gap between the "old" and "modern" schools of photography failed, and he resigned himself to instituting separate juries for pictorial, modern, illustrative, press, and science photography. His crowning achievement was the 1939 salon, which occupied the Education Hall of the American Museum of Natural History for the eight months of the New York World's Fair. The salon's small modern section was lost in a sea of soft-focus pastoral landscapes.[155]

By World War II, the synthesis that White had envisioned—of modern and pictorial, professional and amateur, New York and regional—was shattered. Commercial photographers could no longer communicate with amateurs, and neither group had much that was new to say. Martin's successor as PPA president, Thomas O. Sheckell, captured the mood of the day in "A Broad View," published in *Light and Shade* in March 1939:

> So much is written these days, much of it by newcomers, with little background, but who voice strong arguments. . . . [I]t is not at all convincing but none the less interesting. But what does it matter? We all enjoy our photographic hobby.

This loss of seriousness would have confounded White, for whom photography mattered greatly. White's ambitious amateurism had given way to hobbyism.

In a letter written shortly after White's death, Stieglitz ruminated about his colleague's fate:

> Poor White. Cares and vexation. When I last saw him, he told me he wasn't as able to cope with them as 20 years ago. I reminded him that I warned him to stay in business in Ohio—New York would be too much for him. But the Photo-Secession beckoned. Vanity and ambition. His photography went to the devil—he tried to earn money as a teacher—his pupils—women—half-baked dilettantes—not a single real talent and all for what—a few hellers.[156]

Stieglitz's grim judgments, partly attributable to his misanthropic temperament and sexism, reveal two misunderstandings that have stubbornly endured about White's career. The notion that White was a small-town midwesterner for whom New York was "too much" is widely held. In a 1938 profile of White, journalist Robert W. Marks deliberately contrasted Stieglitz, an avant-garde fighter who "brought Montparnasse to Madison Avenue" with White, "a gentle, Bach-like soul who ma[d]e music almost without meaning to."[157] More recently, Peter Bunnell, White's champion since the 1960s, has attributed the decline in White's art to his "incomplete knowledge" of life in New York.[158]

Although White's manner was unassuming and his art highly personal, he was an intellectually sophisticated man when he came to New York, and he expanded his range of cultural interests once there. White's strength as a teacher was not based solely on his ability to inspire; he gave his students the benefit of his associations with leaders in art, theater, dance, and publishing. White's late photographs, mostly portraits and advertisements, reveal his connections to this cosmopolitan culture. A series of portraits done in 1919 of actress Mae Murray, for example, suggests White's ability to capture the spirit of the jazz age, and a series of nudes from the early 1920s shows his continued exploration of abstraction. Lacking the cohesive vision of the Ohio photographs, White's New York images represent a string of promising but incomplete projects. His greatest enemy in New York was not the city, but his decision to put teaching first.

A second misunderstanding of White's career, so ungenerously noted by Stieglitz, was that White compromised his art merely to support himself. The artist, Stieglitz believed, stood in Olympian isolation from the demands of society, and any attempt to reconcile life's everyday needs with art's higher calling was inherently flawed. By this standard, White's teaching and his advocacy of commercial photography were doomed

from the start. For White, however, the choice between art and society was a false one. White sought common ground between artist and society, a goal as demanding, indeed as utopian, as Stieglitz's.

Despite his oversimplified view of White's character, Robert Marks offers a promising point of departure for a reassessment of White. Marks's 1938 essay on White was the second in a series of twenty-two articles on famous photographers for the fledgling arts magazine *Coronet*.[159] The series was eclectic, including elder statesmen Arnold Genthe, Lejaren à Hiller, and Lewis Hine, as well as younger talents Berenice Abbott, George Platt Lynes, and Alfred Eisenstaedt. The first profile was devoted to Stieglitz, whom Marks labeled a "man with a cause," and the second to White, the "peaceful warrior."[160]

Marks's pairing of Stieglitz and White as the progenitors of modern American photography is significant. White would not be given such prominence today, but in the 1930s, his stature was clear. Moreover, of the twenty-two photographers in Marks's series, sixteen were magazine staff photographers, and some whom Marks deemed important—such as Victor Keppler, who apprenticed to White School teacher Robert Waida and was a pioneer color photographer—are now virtually forgotten. Stieglitz's vision of photography has given rise to the celebration of great art photographers and the neglect of the collaborative but highly creative field of magazine photography. As the magazine era is studied more closely, White is certain to reclaim the central position that he rightly held in his day.

NOTES

See page 201 for short forms of frequently cited sources.

1   John W. Gillies, ed., *Principles of Pictorial Photography* (New York: Falk Publishing Co., 1923), 21; reprinted in Peter C. Bunnell, ed., *A Photographic Vision, Pictorial Photography, 1889–1923* (Salt Lake City: Peregrine Smith, Inc., 1980), 206.

2   Robert W. Marks, "Peaceful Warrior," *Coronet*, vol. 4, no. 6 (October 1938): 161.

3   Letter, Clarence H. White to F. Holland Day, 11 February 1908, Norwood.

4   Letter, Alfred Stieglitz to Heinrich Kühn, 5 August 1925, Stieglitz Archive; Interview, Paul Strand to Maynard P. White Jr., June 1974, cited in *Symbolism of Light*, 20. Among scholars, Peter Bunnell holds this view: see *Reverence*, 17.

5   For example, see Graham Howe, "From Ideal Form to Idealized Fetishism," in *Paul Outerbridge Jr.: Photographs* (New York: Rizzoli, 1980), 9.

6   For a selected bibliography of articles about White, see Bunnell, *Reverence*, 22–23.

7   This comparison was first published by Ronald G. Pisano, *Idle Hours, Americans at Leisure 1865–1914* (Boston: New York Graphic Society, Little Brown & Co., 1988), 68–69.

8   This comparison is reproduced in Barbara L. Michaels, *Gertrude Käsebier, The Photographer and Her Photographs* (New York: Harry N. Abrams, Inc., 1992), 50, 81.

9   Bunnell, *Reverence*, 17.

10   All quotations are from E. O. [sic] Beck, "Newark (Ohio) Exhibition of Pictorial Photography," *Camera Notes*, vol. 4, no. 4 (April 1901): 263–65.

11   See Christian A. Peterson, "American Arts and Crafts: The Photograph Beautiful 1895–1915," in *History of Photography*, vol. 16, no. 3 (Autumn 1992): 189–232.

12   Lorado Taft, "Clarence H. White and the Newark Camera Club," *Brush and Pencil*, vol. 3 (November 1898): cited in *Symbolism of Light*, 14, n. 37.

13   *Camera Work* 3 (July 1903) and *Camera Work* 9 (January 1905); the latter also included an illustration from "Beneath the Wrinkle."

14   Reprinted in Jane Calhoun Weaver, ed., *Sadakichi Hartmann, Critical Modernist* (Berkeley: University of California Press, 1991), 155–62.

15   Steven Marion Reynolds, *Debs: His Life, Writings and Speeches* (Girard, Kansas: The Appeal to Reason, 1908), 74.

16   See M. P. White 1975, 81–82; and *Symbolism of Light*, 18–19. For the Darrow commission, see letter, Clarence H. White to F. Holland Day, 14 May 1904, Norwood.

17   See Eileen Boris, *Art and Labor, Ruskin, Morris, and the Craftsman Ideal in America* (Philadelphia: Temple University Press, 1986).

18   The Camera Club of New York resided at 5 West 31st Street between 1902 and 1907. Its meeting room and darkrooms were on the first floor and its studio, which White later rented, was on the top floor. In 1908 the Camera Club moved to beautiful new headquarters at 121 West 68th Street, where it remained until 1954. For a discussion of Stieglitz's ouster, see Dennis Longwell, "Alfred Stieglitz vs. the Camera Club of New York," *Image*, vol. 14, nos. 5–6 (1971): 21–23.

19   ". . . there are so many exhibitions on here now. The Sirolla's at The Hispanic. The Germans just closed at the Metropolitan, Degas, Arthur B. Davies (Mrs. Käsebier's friend), etchings at both Keppels and Wunderlichs, etc., etc." Letter, Clarence H. White to F. Holland Day, 2 March 1909, Norwood.

20   Letter, Clarence H. White to F. Holland Day, 17 March 1908, Norwood. Edward R. Dickson describes White's studio in his homage to White, "Clarence H. White—A Teacher of Photography," *Photo-Era*, vol. 30, no. 1 (January 1913): 3.

21   Jane Felix White diary, quoted in M. P. White 1975, 284.

22   On two occasions, White complained about his difficulties completing the calendar: Letter, Clarence H. White to F. Holland Day, 13 November 1911 and 1 February 1912, Norwood. "I have some 'ad' work that I have been unable to do because of [teaching]—The business for the photographer has been light they say and this work for 'advertising' is fortunate for me, and I have been able heretofore to please (1 February 1912)." Examples of White's advertising work are in the collections of the Ohio University Gallery of Art and the Art Museum, Princeton University. For published examples, see Bunnell, *Reverence*, 73, and *The Art of Pictorial Photography 1890–1925* (Princeton: The Art Museum, Princeton University), vol. 51, no. 2 (1992): 28.

23   "Society News," *American Photographer*, vol. 1, no. 32 (August 1907): 110.

24   A 1940 chronology, probably drafted by Clarence H. White Jr., specifies that White taught at Columbia until his death in 1925 (White Collection, Princeton).

25   See Frederick C. Moffatt, *Arthur Wesley Dow, 1857–1922* (Washington D.C.: National Collection of Fine Arts, Smithsonian Institution Press, 1977): 49–50, for an excellent discussion of Fenollosa and his influence on Dow.

26   "Training in the Theory and Practice of Teaching Art," *Teacher's College Record*, vol. 9, no. 3 (May 1908): 133.

27   Dow's stamp of approval had lasting value for White. Until 1934 White School brochures opened with a Dow quotation endorsing photography as an art.

28   See Lawrence A. Cremin, et al., *A History of Teachers College, Columbia University* (New York: Columbia University Press, 1954).

29   One Dewey disciple, William Heard Kirkpatrick, was responsible for popularizing the "project method," initially in a 1918 issue of *Teachers College Record*. The *Journal of Educational Method*, founded in 1921, was entirely devoted to the project method debate. See Herbert M. Kliebard, *The Struggle for the American Curriculum 1893–1958* (Boston: Routledge and Kegan Paul, 1986), 156–63.

30   Quotations from Lange cited by M. P. White 1975, 192–94. Despite her praise, Lange was so uninspired by White's assignments that she never completed them!

31   Ibid.

32   For the early history of the Brooklyn Institute, see Rebecca Hooper Eastman, *The Story of The Brooklyn Institute of Arts and Sciences 1824–1924*, published by the Brooklyn Institute in 1924. In 1934 its constituent parts broke into separate institutions, which continue to serve the public today. See also James W. Kent, "The Photographic Department—A History," *The Bulletin of the Brooklyn Institute of Arts and Sciences*, vol. 16, no. 4 (22 April 1916).

33   Letter, Clarence H. White to F. Holland Day, 19 June 1907, Norwood.

34   In her unpublished memoir, "A Photographer's Holiday," p. 45, Jane White describes the economic motivation behind White's summer school. Among the money-saving measures were the sailor suits worn by White and his family, which saved wear and tear on their more expensive city clothes. White Collection, Princeton.

35   "An Article by Arthur Chapman, student of Clarence. Maine. 1910." White Collection, Princeton.

36   Interview, Karl Struss to Susan and John Harvith, 30 August 1975.

37   Letter, Clarence H. White to F. Holland Day, 30 March 1909: "My friend and pupil Mr. Haviland would like to come with me [to visit you at Little Good Harbor, Maine] and he is not certain yet of his movements as the new tarif is likely to affect their business (china). . ." Norwood.

38   See Yochelson, "Karl Struss' New York," in Barbara McCandless, Bonnie Yochelson, and Richard Koszarski, *New York to Hollywood: The Photography of Karl Struss* (Fort Worth: Amon Carter Museum, 1995), 97–123.

39   Letter, White to Stieglitz, June 1907, Stieglitz Archive; Weston J. Naef, *The Collection of Alfred Stieglitz, Fifty Pioneers of Modern Photography* (New York: Metropolitan Museum of Art, 1978), 482.

40   On the Cramer-Thompson series of nudes, see Naef, *The Collection of Alfred Stieglitz*, 490–93. On autochromes, see John Wood, *The Art of the Autochrome, The Birth of Color Photography* (Iowa City: University of Iowa Press, 1993), 62, n. 26.

41   For Käsebier's stormy relationships with her fellow Photo-Secessionists, see Michaels, *Gertrude Käsebier* (note 8 above). In a letter of 25 August 1925 to Heinrich Kühn, Stieglitz claimed that White had been jealous of Steichen (Stieglitz Collection).

42   Clarence H. White to F. Holland Day, 11 February 1908, Norwood.

43   In 1914 Paul L. Anderson described White's central role: "[S]ince the decline of the Photo-Secession, the leadership has been practically vested in Clarence White through his classes, summer school and through his personal attitude toward students." ("The Development of Pictorial Photography in the United States During the Past Quarter Century," *American Photography*, vol. 8, no. 6 [June 1914]: 332, 333).

44   Newark exhibition brochure (6 April to 4 May 1911), Stephen White Collection; photocopy in Struss Collection, Amon Carter Museum, Fort Worth.

45   A copy of the Montross catalogue can be found in Special Collections, New York Public Library.

46   Dow or Weber may have helped arrange for this exhibition. Weber had been commissioned in 1910 to paint Montross's portrait. Although Montross rejected the painting as too distorted, he subsequently gave Weber a major show in 1915.

47   On 19 September 1912, Struss wrote to Stieglitz soliciting photographs for the Montross exhibition. The letter concluded: "I would regret very much not being able to show any of your prints, for, in an exhibition of this character, there is no reason for the sake of good photography why you should not be represented, especially when one considers what you have done for photography" (letter, Karl Struss to Alfred Stieglitz, Stieglitz Archive).

48   See Henry Hope Reed Jr., "Around the Corner to the Little Church," in "Today's Living," *New York Herald Tribune*, 24 June 1962: 2–3.

49   H. G. Wells, *The Door in the Wall and Other Stories*, illustrated with photogravures from photographs by Alvin Langdon Coburn (New York: Mitchell Kennerley, 1911).

50   The Wells commission marked a turning point in Goudy's career. Goudy designed a new typeface for the book, which he named "Kennerley" and which made his reputation as a typographer. Kennerley continued to champion Goudy, commissioning *The Alphabet* (1918) and *Elements of Lettering* (1922), which launched Goudy's career as a teacher of typography. See M. Bruccoli, M. Kennerley, and D. J. R. Bruckner, *Frederic Goudy, Documents of American Design* (New York: Harry N. Abrams, Inc., 1990).

51   "The Terrible Truthfulness of Mr. Shaw," *Camera Work* 29 (January 1910): 17-20.

52   "Fifth Avenue and the Boulevard Saint-Michel," *Forum*, vol. 44 (July–December 1910): 665-85. Kennerley published *Forum* from 1910 to 1916, and Goudy printed it.

53   "Printing in Relation to Advertising," *Barnard's Monographs on Design, Illustration, and Photography* (New York: Charles H. Barnard, July 1912). This pamphlet was designed and printed by Goudy's Village Press and sold by Barnard at 132 Madison Avenue.

54   Laurence J. Gomme, "The Little Book-Shop Around the Corner," *The Colophon* (autumn 1937): 577.

55   *American Photography* (March 1915): 179. The "Notes and News" column announced the monthly meetings at the Little Book-shop of "a very enthusiastic group of photographic workers, without a name or definite organization."

56   The journal listed its office at 2 East 29th Street until the October 1917 issue. That issue, the last, listed the journal's office at 122 East 17th Street, the address of White's school.

57   See Biographies, p. 195; for an obituary of Dickson, see *Pictorial Photography in America*, vol. 3 (1922): 96–97.

58   Augustus Thibaudeau, Spencer Kellogg Jr., and W. H. Porterfield were all distinguished members of the Photo-Pictorialists of Buffalo; Paul L. Anderson was one of the founding teachers at White's school; Arthur D. Chapman and Charles H. Barnard were White students with expertise in printing. Barnard was publisher of *Platinum Print* for its first two issues; he then moved to Montreal, where he continued to participate in White's activities as a PPA regional representative.

59   Paul L. Anderson, "Development of Pictorial Photography in the United States During the Past Quarter Century," *American Photography*, vol. 8 (1914): 332.

60   Gomme, "Little Book-Shop Around the Corner," 577.

61   The review was reprinted in *Platinum Print*, vol. 1, no. 3 (March 1914): 5. Stieglitz wrote to Steichen, "I suppose you have gotten the amusing White invitation to the Photographic Show. I got one and am going to ignore it. I have no two cent stamp to waste on it. Money is too scarce" (4 December 1913, Stieglitz Archive).

62   Letter to Stieglitz from the committee organizing the Rosenbach Gallery exhibition, 23 October 1914, Stieglitz Archive; see the review of Rosenbach exhibition by Maurice T. Fleisher, *Platinum Print*, vol. 2, no. 1 (1915): 4.

63   On 15 January 1916, a formal meeting was held at the offices of Dr. Charles H. Jaeger, a White student and the husband of Doris Ulmann. A committee consisting of Walter Ehrich, Dickson, Struss, White, and another White student, Mary B. White, was formed to draw up a constitution for the PPA ("The Call," *Pictorial Photographers of America* [1917]: 8).

64   Struss to Susan and John Harvith, 12 September 1975. In the 1930s, when the early years of the PPA acquired a mythical status, many versions of its founding circulated. Paul Anderson, for example, claimed that the idea for a national organization originated at the 1916 summer session. Dr. D. J. Ruzicka, a member of the first executive committee, claimed that the PPA was initially discussed at his home. The idea for

a national organization was no doubt "in the air" and discussed on many occasions.

65   See "Pictorial Photographs of America, Its Work and Its Aim," *Photo=Graphic Art*, vol. 3, no. 2 (October 1917): 18; this final issue of *Photo=Graphic Art* includes the PPA's initial list of officers and members.

66   White was listed as a juror for the AIGA's *Exhibition of American Printing* in 1916 and 1920.

67   Art Alliance of America and AIGA, *Graphic Arts: Advertisements, Catalogues, Color Printing, Containers, Labels, Letterheads, Lithographs, Magazine Covers, Pamphlets, Photographs, Posters, and Wrappers*, Second Annual Exhibition, 30 April–24 May 1919.

68   "We had no association of any kind with the local camera clubs. We were more associated with the unorganized Photo-Secession which Stieglitz headed at the time." Karl Struss to John and Susan Harvith, 12 September 1975. In a *Platinum Print* editorial, Dickson chastised the camera clubs: ". . . the motive for your existence seems more largely sustained by the impetus derived from annual exhibitions of the conventional in photography than by love of progress and new expressions" ("Editorially Expressed: Our Camera Clubs: Their Opportunities," vol. 1, no. 6 [November 1914]: 3).

69   For a list of participating organizations, see *Photo=Graphic Art*, vol. 3, no. 2 (October 1917): 22.

70   M. P. White 1975, 213; and *Symbolism of Light*, 24–25.

71   In her diary, Jane White lamented the poor condition of the 11th Street house: "Pay rent and ask for nothing for you won't get it, is their policy" (M. P. White 1975, 180). Reverend Guthrie is listed on the advisory board and as a speaker in the 1914 White School brochure. White Collection, Princeton.

72   "Mr. Goudy I have been able to get better acquainted with, and he has asked to do a book around some of my photographs. . . . I am adding to my portraits of the dancers and a little volume on dancing I hope will materialize." White to Day, 1 February 1912, Norwood.

73   Christopher Gray, "The Washington Irving House: Why the Legend of Irving Place Is But a Myth," *New York Times* (13 March 1994): 7.

74   Paul L. Anderson, "Some Pictorial History," *American Photography*, vol. 29, no. 4 (April 1935): 210.

75   Memo from Richard M. Coit, chairman of the department of photography, Brooklyn Institute of Arts and Sciences, 28 September 1916, Struss Archive, Amon Carter Museum. For Anderson, see Terence R. Pitts, "Paul Lewis Anderson: A Life in Photography," *The Archive*, Center for Creative Photography, University of Arizona, Research Series, no. 18 (May 1983).

76   H. R. Poore, *Pictorial Composition and the Critical Judgement of Pictures*, 1903. As a Paris-trained academician, Poore served as artistic mentor to the self-taught Anderson.

77   For a summary of Anderson's theory, see Pitts, "Anderson."

78   "The Reminiscences of Max Weber," interviewed by Carol S. Gruber, Oral History Research Office, Columbia University, 1958, 96.

79   Weber's manuscript is in the Stieglitz Archive. In "A Photographer's Holiday" (p. 45), Jane White wrote that Weber was "our first art instructor." White Collection, Princeton.

80   "The Filling of Space," *Platinum Print*, vol. 1, no. 2 (December 1913): 6; "Tradition and Now," *Photo=Graphic Art*, vol. 3, no. 1 (June 1916): 11.

81   In the collection of Weber's daughter Joy are portraits by Chapman, Sipprell, and Horne, as well as by Struss and Anderson. Many more are unsigned.

82   "The Filling of Space" (see note 80).

83   Ibid.

84   Weber, "Reminiscences," 276 (see note 78).

85   Weber, "Design" (paragraph accompanying four design exercises), *Photo=Graphic Art*, vol. 3, no. 1 (June 1916): 8.

86   This print had belonged to Margaret Watkins. On Giridlian, see Jane White letter to Day, 26 January 1917, Norwood; and "Photographer's Holiday," 100.

87   Coburn planned to visit New York in 1914, but apparently did not cross the Atlantic after war broke out in Europe. He must have fulfilled his obligation to White's school by correspondence in 1914, because his critique was again listed in 1915. His selection of White student works for the 1915 RPS exhibition was most likely made from work sent to England for his review.

88   *Photograms of the Year*, vol. 12 (1916), 23–24; reprinted in Bunnell, ed., *Photographic Vision*, 194–95 (see note 1).

89   "Notes and News," *American Photography* (March 1915): 179, mentions Strand among those who attended a Weber print critique at the Little Book-shop.

90   Laura Gilpin, *American Annual of Photography*, vol. 40 (1926): 154.

91   *Greenwich Village, Eight Portraits by Arthur D. Chapman* (New York: Philip Goodman Co.), 1915.

92   Chapman, "Travel," *American Annual of Photography* (1918), 238.

93   Letter, Chapman to Robert W. G. Vail, director, 3 January 1952, Prints and Photographs Department, New-York Historical Society.

94   Pictorial Photographers of America, *Annual Report* (National Arts Club, 1918), 14.

95   Ibid.

96   Walter Hervey, president of Teachers College from 1891 to 1897, was an active member of White's circle. He was president of the Clarence H. White Realty Company, and he lectured at the school on "the psychology of art."

97   In the spring of 1921, Hervey gave a lecture, "Photography as a Career for Women," in connection with a traveling exhibition that opened at Hunter College of photographs by alumnae of the White School (*The Bulletin of the Alumni*, Clarence H. White School of Photography, Spring & Summer Number [June 1921]: unpaginated).

98   This phrase is used in all White School brochures.

99   Some of these photographers are discussed by Naomi Rosenblum in *A History of Women Photographers* (New York: Abbeville Press, 1995).

100   White printed special catalogues for these two courses, "Printing and Photography Related," and "A Professional Course for the Professional Worker" (White Collection, Princeton).

101   For Sipprell, see McCabe, *Clara Sipprell*; for Gilpin, see Sandweiss, *An Enduring Grace*; and for Ulmann, see Featherstone, *Doris Ulmann: American Portraits* (Albuquerque: University of New Mexico Press, 1985).

102   M. P. White 1975, 204.

103   Paul Hill and Thomas Cooper, eds., *Dialogue with Photography* (New York: Farrar Straus Giroux, 1979), 285.

104   For a succinct discussion of "the new woman," see Lois Rudnick, "The New Woman," in *1915, The Cultural Moment*, Adele Heller and Lois Rudnick, eds. (New Brunswick: Rutgers University Press, 1991), 69–81.

105   In 1916 the Brooklyn Institute's photography classes were cross-listed as extension school courses for the department of pedagogy. White's success at Columbia's Teachers College may have prompted the institute to offer his courses to its own education students (*The Twenty-ninth Year Book of The Brooklyn Institute of Arts and Sciences* [1918], 126).

106   A brochure (from after 1920) describing White's practice notes: "Mr. White was the first to make portraits in home surroundings" (White Collection, Princeton).

107   Clarence H. White, "Photography as a Profession for Women," *American Photography*, vol. 18, no. 7 (July 1924): 428.

108   Ibid., 432.

109   The neighborhood acquired the name "Sugar Hill" during White's years, when it attracted luminaries of the Harlem Renaissance, including Duke Ellington, Langston Hughes, Paul Robeson, and W. E. B. Dubois.

110   *The Bulletin of the Alumni*, Housewarming number, December 1920, no pagination, White Collection, Princeton.

111   Whether White completed the twenty portfolios of ten prints each is unknown.

112   Letter, F. R. Fraprie to White, 10 October 1922, White Collection, Princeton.

113   Stieglitz to Heinrich Kühn, 25 August 1925, Stieglitz Archive.

114   Jane White to F. Holland Day, 24 March 1926, Norwood.

115   "A Letter from Clarence White," *Abel's Photographic Weekly*, vol. 32, no. 824 (6 October 1923): 386, 388.

116   In 1915 Martin taught a new course at Teachers College on "modernist painting," which was instituted to keep abreast of "the tendencies of the times." See Moffatt, *Arthur Wesley Dow*, 122 (note 25). When Dow died, in 1922, Martin became chairman of the department of fine arts at Teachers College.

117   The lectures were first offered in 1920 at the Washington Irving House.

118   In a letter of 11 January 1922, Stieglitz confirmed his commitment to talk at the school (Stieglitz Archive), and the school lecture list for the fall 1923–24 semester lists Stieglitz for 8 February 1924. For a summary of Stieglitz's talk at the Art Center, see "A Stieglitz Talk at a New York Art Center," *The Center for Creative Photography*, Tucson, Arizona, no. 1 (March 1976): 1–8.

119   Strand's talk took place on 23 March 1923. "The Art Motive in Photography" was originally published *British Journal of Photography*, vol. 70 (5 October 1923): 612–14; for a reprint, see Vicki Goldberg, ed., *Photography in Print, Writings from 1816 to the Present* (New York: Simon and Schuster, 1981), 276–87.

120   The *Vanity Fair* features were as follows: Sheeler, "Cubist Architecture in New York," January 1921: 72; Bruguière, "A Modernist Setting for the New Production of Macbeth," April 1921: 46; "Experiments in Modernistic Photography, Ira Martin Attempts to Solve with the Camera Some of the Problems which Confront the Cubist Painter," July 1921: 60; "Photography Comes into the Kitchen, A Group of Photographs by Margaret Watkins Showing Modernist, or Cubist, Patterns in Composition," October 1921: 60; Outerbridge, "The Kitchen Table, A Study in Ellipses, Suggesting How the Modern Conception of Abstract Design May Be Applied to Still Life," July 1922: 52; "Experiments in Abstract Form, Made Without a Camera Lens by Man Ray, The American Painter," November 1922: 50.

121   Helen Sargent Hitchcock (1870–1938) was the young widow of Ripley Hitchcock, art critic and editor. In 1914 she founded the Art Alliance of America (AAA) to help women find employment in the arts.

122   White belonged to several of the seven societies: AAA, AIGA, PPA, and the

Stowaways. The Stowaways was a social club for book and print aficionados, with Goudy and his friends at its core.

123 For White's role in the history of the *Art Center Bulletin*, see *Art Center Bulletin*, vol. 9, no. 1 (October 1930): p. 3.

124 The National Arts Club was founded in 1898. According to its mission statement, it aimed at "the promotion of the arts and crafts, in order ultimately to improve the quality of our manufactures; and stimulate interest in the embellishment of cities and public buildings."

125 For discussions of the early years of advertising from the "creative" point of view, see Roland Marchand, *Advertising the American Dream, Making Way for Modernity, 1920–1940* (Berkeley: University of California Press, 1985); and Michele Bogart, *Artists, Advertising, and the Borders of Art* (Chicago: University of Chicago Press, 1995): 125–69 (chapter 3).

126 Quoted by Egbert G. Jacobson in Art Directors Club, *Annual of Advertising Art in the United States*, vol. 1 (1921): ix.

127 "Of Ideas," *Pictorial Photography in America*, vol. 3 (1922), 13–14.

128 From a report on Campbell's talk at the Art Center, *Art Center Bulletin*, vol. 1, no. 1 (September 1924): 14.

129 Helen Appleton Read, "Notes on the Exposition des Arts Decoratifs," *Art Center Bulletin*, vol. 4, no. 6 (February 1926): 171.

130 Marchand, *Advertising the American Dream*, 140–48.

131 *Art Center Bulletin*, vol. 3, no. 7 (March 1925): 172–76. The article was reprinted without illustrations in *Commercial Photographer*, vol. 1, no. 4 (January 1926): 128–31.

132 Ibid.

133 Art Directors Club, *Annual of Advertising Art in the United States*, vol. 3 (1924), no pagination.

134 "Advertising and Photography," *Pictorial Photography in America*, vol. 4 (1926), no pagination.

135 Stieglitz to Heinrich Kühn, 25 August 1925, Stieglitz Archive.

136 Jane Felix White to F. Holland Day, 29 November 1925, Jane Felix White Papers, Norwood Historical Society, Norwood, Massachusetts.

137 Jane Felix White to F. Holland Day, 24 March 1926, Norwood.

138 M. M. Wardell, of Wills & Wardell to Mrs. Jane F. White, 7 September 1926, White Collection, Princeton.

139 Brenda Putnam, Gilpin's lifelong friend, was the daughter of Herbert Putnam, the librarian of Congress. At Gilpin's urging, Putnam acquired a selection of White's photographs for the library.

140 Stanley Resor, "Ending the Isolation of Specialization, An Immediate Job If America Is to Produce the Next Great Renascence of Art," *Art Center Bulletin*, vol. 5, no. 8 (April 1927): 139–40. For Steichen, see "Minutes of the Representatives Meetings," (31 January 1928): 2–3 (J. Walter Thompson Archives, Duke University), cited in Patricia Johnston, *Real Fantasies: Edward Steichen's Advertising Photographs* (Berkeley: University of California Press, forthcoming), chapter 2.

141 Johnston, *Real Fantasies*, chapter 6.

142 Phyllis Dearborn Massar, interview with the author, 15 February 1994.

143 Brochures for the New York Institute of Photography list a wide range of courses for still and motion picture photography taught at three locations: 141 W. 36th Street in Manhattan's photo district; 505 State Street, opposite the Long Island train terminal; and 630 South Wabash Avenue, Chicago.

144 A resumé for Clarence H. White Jr., in the White Collection, Princeton, states that "the Clarence H. White School of Photography was accredited by the University of the State of New York."

145 Steichen to Helen Simmons, 14 May 1938, collection of Helen Simmons Faye.

146 Just as Jane White had done, Ruth White, Clarence Jr.'s wife, ran the school's office, and the family continued to live on the school's top floor. Relationships between staff, students, and the Whites remained familial (interview by author with Phyllis D. Massar, 2 February 1994).

147 The bulletin, renamed *White with Detail*, provides thorough information about the school's last two years.

148 "I had gone back to work at Macy's because the school was unable to pay my salary and, in fact, they owed both Mert and me some back wages. Clarence called us to come over to the school and select a print of his father's to make up for the money owed us. I chose the portrait of Alfred Stieglitz which was eventually sold in 1985 for $37,400 at Christie's"; Helen Simmons Faye to Kathleen Erwin, letter of August 20, 1993.

149 The Utility of Beauty in Advertising," *Art Center Bulletin*, vol. 4, no. 1 (September 1925): 6.

150 *Art Center Bulletin*, vol. 9, no. 6 (March 1931).

151 The director of the New York Regional Art Council was Florence Nightingale Levy, who in 1914 had founded the Art Alliance of America with Helen Sargent Hitchcock. After ten years as director of the Baltimore Museum of Art, Levy returned to New York in 1927 to lead the Art Council.

152 National Alliance of Art & Industry, New York Regional Art Council, *Minutes 1927–1932*. The last issue of *Art Center Bulletin* (vol. 9, no. 9 [November–December 1931]) announced, under the euphemistic headline "Art Center Changes," the dissolution of the federation of the center's seven organizations. In October 1932 it held an "Exhibition of Photographs for Art and Industry," jointly sponsored by the PPA and the National Alliance of Art & Industry (brochure in the White Collection, Princeton), and in April 1933 it still hosted the Art Directors Club annual exhibition of advertising art.

153 *Light and Shade* as a printed bulletin ran from October 1928 to May 1932. By April 1933, it had been replaced by a four-page mimeographed newsletter, *Bulletin of the Pictorial Photographers of America*. In October 1937, when Samuel Grierson assumed editorship, the mimeographed newsletter returned to the name *Light and Shade*; Grierson remained editor until 1953.

154 From 1937 to 1939, Thomas O. Sheckell served as the PPA's president. Although more conservative than Martin, he was still interested in modern trends. After 1940 the PPA functioned like other camera clubs, with no special interest in New York art or commercial photographers.

155 *Light and Shade* documents the annual salons from 1937 to 1941.

156 Letter, Alfred Stieglitz to Heinrich Kühn, 25 August 1925, Stieglitz Collection, Beinecke Library of Rare Books and Manuscripts, Yale University.

157 Marks, "Peaceful Warrior" (note 2 above): 161.

158 Bunnell, *Reverence*, 17.

159 *Coronet* was a Chicago-based arts magazine edited by Arnold Gingrich and published by David A. Smart. Begun in November 1936, it regularly ran portfolios of American and European photographs, and, in addition to Marks's profiles, introduced a column of interviews with photographers called "Talking Pictures."

160 "Man With A Cause, Many a Drowsy Worshipper Nodded Outside Until Alfred Stieglitz Opened Wide the Door," *Coronet*, vol. 4, no. 5 (September 1938): 161–70. For a full citation of the article on White, see note 2.

"PHOTOGRAPHY OF THE BETTER TYPE"

THE TEACHING OF CLARENCE H. WHITE

Kathleen A. Erwin

CLARENCE H. WHITE (1871–1925) INTRODUCED COMPREHENSIVE INSTRUCTION IN ART PHOTOGRAPHY IN THE UNITED STATES.

He taught hundreds of students, in New York City, Maine, and Connecticut. The Clarence H. White School of Photography, which he founded in New York City in 1914 and which flourished until 1942, was the only school in the United States wholly devoted to instruction in art photography. White was clearly an inspiring teacher, through the charisma of his personality and his dedication to the principles and value of art. He cultivated in his students their perception and appreciation of art, so that they might "enjoy the happiness of better work" and possibly even earn their living creating "photography of the better type."[1] He strongly advocated studying and practicing design in photography; in his school, he always had one other instructor concentrate on teaching principles of design.

A number of White's students created photographs that were immediately celebrated and influential. While some of these students enjoy established positions in photography history, others of these once-celebrated artists have been forgotten. At least several of the latter produced impressive bodies of work that also deserve a place in the history of photography.

Jane Felix White (1869–1943), Clarence White's wife, remembered that shortly after their marriage in 1893, "almost as soon as he had accomplished results in the first attempts with his small Kodak, he had gotten his friends interested in trying their hands at photography, and he disclosed to them every new step as he acquired it."[2] Although White was employed as a bookkeeper, his gifts as a natural teacher thus became obvious even before he produced the photographs that would bring him international recognition.

White was motivated to make the decisive transition from taking snapshots to being a pictorial, or artistic, photographer by a lecture in 1896 on composition in photography by O. Walter Beck, a painter and teacher at the Art Academy of Cincinnati. Beck introduced White to "the world of possibilities in photography for the artist" and inspired him to "at once set to work trying to make his photographs pictures," or, in other words, art.[3]

THE NEWARK (OHIO) CAMERA CLUB: THE FIRST "WHITE SCHOOL"

In 1898 the Newark Camera Club was founded in White's hometown, Newark, Ohio, and White became its president and leader. Later that year, photographs by White shown in the first Philadelphia salon, the first photography exhibition to be sponsored by a recognized American art institution, were so well received that he was asked to be a member of the jury for the next Philadelphia salon in 1899; his fellow jurors included photographers F. Holland Day and Gertrude Käsebier. Thus, Clarence White made the connections that allowed the Newark Camera Club—although distant from the major cities that were the established centers of artistic photography—to present in 1899 and 1900 outstanding exhibitions that included the work of such prominent art photographers as Day, Käsebier, and Alfred Stieglitz.

Ema Spencer, a member, published an article on the Newark Camera Club in the July 1901 *Camera Craft*. Spencer noted that the club was "known in photographic circles here and abroad as the 'White School'," a statement reflecting both the group's international prominence and White's importance to it. She reported that White had "a large fund of helpfulness and suggestiveness always at the service of those who have been stimulated by his sustained enthusiasm, or, in fact, of any who ask it," and that his mentoring of his fellow club members was "the natural outcome of the influence of a strong nature over those of similar tastes and lesser abilities," but with "the work of each member being independent and the individuality of each respected and fostered."

In her article, Spencer also acknowledged the club's debt to principles promoted by O. Walter Beck, who had first inspired Clarence White to practice photography as an art. Spencer noted that the members thoroughly endorsed "Professor Beck's postulate that 'art is above all things an interpreter of the artist's character, his emotion, his intellectual powers, and it is his nature that the finished photograph must reveal.'" Beck had published this statement in the April 1901 *Camera Notes*, in which he also wrote: "Art *can* be brought into photography and it *can* be taught!" Clarence White, as if inspired by Beck's article—as he was by Beck's lecture—wrote to Alfred Stieglitz on 17 April 1901: "I have made up my mind that art in photography will be my life work."[4]

*Ethel Wall Struss Seated
under Two Trees, 1921*

In her article in *Camera Craft*, Spencer further reflected on Beck's influence: "One of the vital principles in the creed of the 'White School' is that 'art *can* be brought into photography.'" She continued:

> It is surprising how little talk there is in this club of formulae, lenses and shutters, of mechanical processes and media. The art spirit is so predominant that the meetings resemble more those of a body of art students than those of a camera club. . . . "The eye only beholds what it brings the capacity to see." The constant exhortation of Mr. White to those who are glad to profit by his counsel is toward the cultivation of this "capacity to see."

PICTORIAL PHOTOGRAPHY AND THE PHOTO-SECESSION

During White's lifetime, "pictorial photography" meant "art photography" or "artistic photography," terms that were also frequently used. White himself defined pictorial photography in 1918 as photography with "construction and expression."[5] In the first decades of the century, just as today, the great majority of photographs taken were without such artistic intent—they were amateur snapshots, for example, or scientific or commercial records of objects. The very newness of the concept was an added stumbling block to the recognition of photography as a potential medium of art. To promote the recognition of pictorial photography as a distinct means of individual espression, the group known as the Photo-Secession was begun in 1902 by Alfred Stieglitz, with White as one of the founding members.

WHITE'S FIRST FORMAL TEACHING POSITION: COLUMBIA UNIVERSITY

In 1904 White somewhat precipitously left the security of his position of bookkeeper in Newark, only to become disillusioned with supporting his family as an itinerant portrait photographer and photographic illustrator. In 1906 he moved to New York City, where he hoped to support his family through photography and also be in closer contact with the leaders of the Photo-Secession.[6]

In January 1907, not yet settled in New York, White wrote to F. Holland Day: "I am realizing that my education of the public must be drawing to a close. I am doing nothing with my camera and my long effort—since 1898—to help the cause has about wound up the ball for me."[7] That year, however, far from seeing the end of White's educational efforts, marked the beginning of his professional career as a teacher. As lecturer in fine arts in extension teaching at Columbia University, he taught a newly introduced course in art photography from 1907 to 1910 and became a lecturer for Teachers College, Columbia University, from 1910 until his death in 1925.[8] A special detailed prospectus of 1911

described White's courses at Teachers College as devoted to photography as a medium of individual expression, and as qualifying students as photographers practicing in portraiture, illustration, architecture, trades, or the professions.[9]

By more than one account, Alfred Stieglitz had been instrumental in White's appointment. Many years later, Stieglitz recollected that Arthur Wesley Dow, director of the department of fine arts at Teachers College, had proposed that Stieglitz teach a photography course at Columbia. Stieglitz suggested White for the job instead, saying that White would make an excellent teacher.[10] Years later, in 1942, Jane White noted that Alfred Stieglitz had recently commented that White had always been a teacher, even before Stieglitz "recommended him to Columbia University."[11] She remembered urging her husband to teach at Columbia: "You *know*, Clarence, you have a message. And after all, that's what teaching really is. You'll just have to teach."[12]

It indeed came about that Dow encouraged Teachers College art students "to study design with the camera in order to avail themselves of the excellent training in composition" that White's course offered.[13] Margaret Bourke-White took Clarence White's photography course during her freshman year at Columbia (1921–22) just because of its emphasis on design.[14] From 1911 on, photography students at Teachers College were encouraged also to take a general course in design. An exhibition room allowed for the "annual showing of student work and for the display of the work of prominent photographers."[15]

In June 1907 White had informed F. Holland Day of his appointment, saying that he thought his teaching at Columbia would be of great value to him in experience and that he trusted he might be able to give a little to those entering the class.[16] White left unmentioned the attraction of the income he would receive without having to travel more than a few blocks away from his family. White wrote Day in February 1908, "My class gives the closest attention. I hate though to look to the future and see myself a dried up teacher of photography. But I guess that is the only cog I've even started in this year[']s wheel."[17] A statement by White in 1923, however, made his career choice sound more purposeful. He wrote of when photography became his full-time profession, in 1904:

> Photography then became my real work, but I was still anxious to keep the attitude of the amateur by doing the best in me. I believed in photography as an *expression for an artist*. This persistence led me into another field of photography, that of teaching.[18]

For White, teaching was preferable to commercial photography because it provided income while allowing him to promote artistic expression in photography to an ever-increasing circle: at Columbia, he trained teachers, who in turn disseminated what they had learned across the country.

White's Teaching Extended:
Brooklyn Institute of Arts and Sciences

For the school years 1908–09 and 1909–10, the second and third of White's three-year appointment as lecturer in extension teaching at Columbia, the Columbia University *Announcement of Extension Teaching* listed White's art photography class as also being offered at the Brooklyn Institute of Arts and Sciences.[19] The institute, where White continued to teach until 1922, offered a wide range of continuing education programs. Previously—from 1894 to 1903—the institute's department of photography had offered classes that included instruction in "artistic posing and lighting."[20] In 1908, after its move to more comfortable quarters in the new Brooklyn Academy of Music on Lafayette Avenue, it held two evening courses in artistic photography, one intermediate and one advanced, taught by "Clarence H. White, of Columbia University."[21] In 1909 the *Bulletin of The Brooklyn Institute of Arts and Sciences* reported that

> The classes . . . were more or less informal, the members being at liberty to ask questions in order to obtain information required by their individual needs. . . . It is Mr. White's aim to encourage and direct the work of the members along the lines in which they show themselves best adapted, believing that in this way individual expression in photography is best secured.[22]

The department regularly offered short exhibitions of the work of distinguished photographers as well as of its members.

Seguinland School of Photography, Georgetown, Maine

Before and after their move to New York City, Clarence and Jane White and their sons had made visits to F. Holland Day's summer home on Georgetown Island, Maine, visits they enjoyed immensely. In early 1910 the Whites bought an old house on Sheepscot Bay, near Day's. According to Jane White, in Maine her husband and their sons lived in sailor suits, flannel for cold days, cotton for warm days, thereby saving wear and tear on their town clothes. Even with this economy, however, they still needed an income, so Clarence decided, "as a solution to this problem of finances," to open a summer school of photography.[23] That summer, "in answer to requests for more thorough training than that offered by Columbia and Brooklyn Institute," White founded the Seguinland School of Photography, named for its locale on Georgetown Island.[24] Doubtless, both willing students and White's need for income prompted him to offer summer classes. The first year, eight students came, from New York, Baltimore, Philadelphia, Chicago, California, Ecuador, and Egypt.[25] As can be seen in some of the pictures they made, many of the summer students, like the Whites, dressed in sailor suits, which were both utilitarian and served to homogenize the group.

From 1910 to 1915 White offered summer photography courses on Georgetown Island.[26] School catalogues described the area's "storm-beaten cliffs, bold headlands, islands and rocks, hard, clean sand beaches, salt rivers & lagoons, lakes, brooks and woods." Each summer, the work of well-known photographers was exhibited and that of the class itself at the end of the session. F. Holland Day critiqued student work at his summer home regularly during the school's annual tenure in Maine.[27] In addition, Gertrude Käsebier critiqued student work during a visit in 1913;[28] she was also listed as a special lecturer in the following year's New York City school catalogue. Like White, Käsebier was a founding member of the Photo-Secession. She ran a profitable portrait studio and her photographs were well known through their reproduction in magazines. Correspondence of Jane White from 1927 and 1930 attests to Käsebier's continuing interest in White School students. Jane White reported on a class visit to Käsebier in 1930: "They had a delightful hour or two with her. She showed them her portfolio—& talked, as you remember she can, so entertainingly, & they had a wonderful time."[29]

THE CLARENCE H. WHITE SCHOOL OF PHOTOGRAPHY, NEW YORK

In October 1914 the Clarence H. White School of Photography began operation at 230 East 11th Street, which simultaneously became the Whites' residence. The trustees of the neighboring St. Mark's-in-the-Bouwerie owned the property. The school would continue at this and three successive New York City venues until 1942.

The August 1914 issue of *Platinum Print*, edited by White's close associate Edward Dickson, announced the impending opening of the school. A notice, under the title "A New School of Photography," read:

> The Clarence H. White School of Photography at [230] East 11th Street, New York, will open its doors in October. It is founded as an institution for teaching the science and art of photography and for the training of its students for the vocation of photographer. The school will afford every facility for experiment and practice under constructive criticism of its principal. The special lectures on art are intended to acquaint the student with the principles of art appreciation and to enable him to use his medium for expressing his aesthetic sense. Mr. Max Weber, the lecturer on art, is recognized in Europe and in the United States as a distinguished artist and an able exponent of plastic art. The technical demonstrations by Mr. Paul L. Anderson are intended to instruct the student in the chemistry of photography and the laws which govern lenses and their employment. Mr. Anderson is an acknowledged authority and writer on these subjects. One of the features of the school will be periodical visits to the Metropolitan Museum of Art where the students will hear lec-

MARY LACY VAN WAGENEN
Summer Session, Clarence H. White
School of Photography, Canaan,
Connecticut, 1917

DOROTHEA LANGE
Ex-Slave with a Long Memory,
Alabama, 1937

139

tures on distinguished art objects. Mr. Clarence H. White, the principal, is a lecturer on art photography at the Columbia University and the Brooklyn Institute of Arts.

Advertisements for, and other references to the school in *Platinum Print* during 1914 and 1915 (fig. 14), as well as the catalogue for White's sixth summer session in Maine, 1915, gave the name of the school as the "Clarence H. White School of Modern Photography," but "Modern" was dropped from the name sometime in 1915.[30]

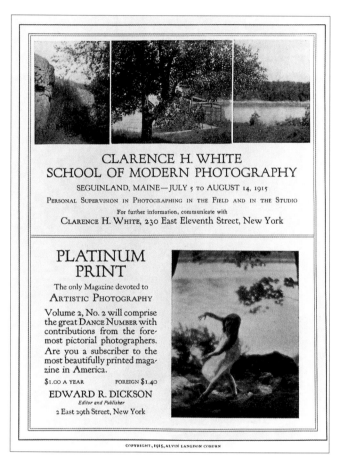

CLARENCE H. WHITE
SCHOOL OF MODERN PHOTOGRAPHY
SEGUINLAND, MAINE—JULY 5 TO AUGUST 14, 1915
PERSONAL SUPERVISION IN PHOTOGRAPHING IN THE FIELD AND IN THE STUDIO
For further information, communicate with
CLARENCE H. WHITE, 230 East Eleventh Street, New York

PLATINUM PRINT
The only Magazine devoted to
ARTISTIC PHOTOGRAPHY

Volume 2, No. 2 will comprise the great DANCE NUMBER with contributions from the foremost pictorial photographers. Are you a subscriber to the most beautifully printed magazine in America.

$1.00 A YEAR   FOREIGN $1.40

EDWARD R. DICKSON
Editor and Publisher
2 East 29th Street, New York

COPYRIGHT, 1915, ALVIN LANGDON COBURN

(figure 14)

UNIDENTIFIED PHOTOGRAPHER
Platinum Print, *vol. 2, no. 1 (1915): inside front cover*

According to the school's 1914 and 1915 catalogues, "New York City is the metropolis and art centre of the United States. It is the one city, therefore, where such an institution as this finds its fit and proper location." While photography was taught elsewhere in the country, concentration on the teaching of pictorial or art photography made the White School unique. It taught art history, design, and photographic technique as part of a cohesive single program, rather than just the technical aspects of photography typically taught to scientists. In 1919 White claimed that his school's variety of training "will enable the student to pursue his photographic work and art training in one school— an educational convenience offered by no other institution in this country."[31] The 1914 catalogue continued:

In the past decade, photography has taken so important a place in the industrial as well as in the fine arts that an institute devoted to its instruction and practice has become a matter of immediate necessity. In almost every department of industrial activity and human enterprise, in travel and the records of science, in the publishing of books and the dissemination of knowledge, photography either plays an indispensable part or is destined to play such part in the near future. . . . The School is open to men and women . . . . The course of instruction requires the entire time of the student in lectures and practical work for the period of thirty weeks.

Throughout its history, the White School specifically mentioned in the catalogues for its New York City classes that it was "open to men and women"—though it never made the same statement in its summer school catalogues. It is worth noting that among Clarence White's known students, there are roughly twice as many women as men. The 1915 school catalogue included a "post graduate course," added to accommodate students who wanted to continue their training at the school.

STELLA F. SIMON

Exhibition and Lecture Room,
Clarence H. White School of
Photography, 460 W. 144th
Street, New York, ca. 1924

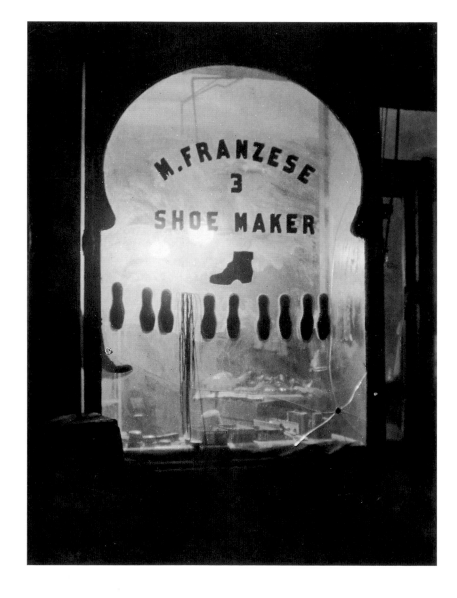

TEACHERS AND COURSES

Of the thirty school hours each week during the 1914–15 school year, fourteen were devoted to "The Art of Photography," taught by White. The 1914 and 1915 catalogues listed a page of subtopics to be covered by White, including the discovery and development of photography; selection of point of view in photographing; the educational value of photography; commercial photography—photography for advertising and illustration; and street and newspaper photography.

For six hours each week, Paul Anderson taught "Technique of Photography," which the catalogue described as including numerous print processes: commercial and hand-coated platinum, silver, printing out and gaslight, single and multiple carbon, single and multiple gum, oil, bromoil, and photogravure. Anderson, a respected master of the technical aspects of photography, not only relieved White of the burden of attending to technical matters but also reinforced White's teaching of art photography, of which Anderson was a productive theoretician and a fervent promoter. In "Where Are We to Get Our Pictorialists?" he noted "By technique I mean not merely knowledge of how to use . . . apparatus but also facility of observation and skill in composition."[32] In another article, "The Education of the Photographic Artist," Anderson maintained that encouraging harmonious development "can best be done by criticizing each of the student's prints for the three essentials—thought, design and technique—and by impressing on him the necessity for employing all three in each instance."[33]

From his lectures at the White School, Anderson developed *Pictorial Photography, Its Principles and Practice*, a book on photographic technique first published in 1917. He continued as a recognized authority on photographic technique, notably as a prolific writer, after he left the White School in 1918 and on into the 1940s.

Max Weber (1881–1961), an avant-garde modernist painter and former student of Arthur Wesley Dow, taught "Art Appreciation and Design" at the school from 1914 to 1918. Weber was pivotal in introducing the New York art world to what he had learned of modern art in Europe while studying in Paris from 1905 to 1908, championing Cézanne in particular. Weber contributed strongly to the White School's credo of design in photography. Over forty years later, he reminisced about the beginning of his teaching at the school:

> [White] began to see my exhibitions. And he asked me to take charge of the art, such as composition and design, and I said, 'To really pursue the life of an artist, you must know the history of art.' So it was agreed that I should lecture on the history of art thirty consecutive weeks, and I would go to the Metropolitan Museum every Tuesday afternoon . . . and spend three or four hours selecting my slides. It wasn't an academic lecture at all.

JOSEPHINE M. WALLACE
Canaan Doorway, ca. 1920

For instance, say, I got to the Dutch school, to mention Rembrandt. I did not adhere to only slides of Rembrandt's art. Since it was a question of design and composition, or a question of plastic values, or the canons of art, I would bring in a musical instrument, say, a Hindu instrument, which was fantastic in design. I would bring in a Chinese rug and show that it was the same thing, a Rembrandt or a canvas by Mantegna—that design was design. And such was the nature of my talks.[34]

In this way, Weber stimulated in his students what White had exhorted the Newark Camera Club to cultivate, the "capacity to see." Weber wanted his students to perceive the composition of their own environment, as well as that of art masterworks. Moreover, he drilled his students to be disciplined in creating their own compositions in drawn and photographic exercises. The 1915 school catalogue gave more details of Weber's weekly Wednesday instruction:

> The lectures on art appreciation are given in the morning hours of the first half of this course; the same hours of the second half of the school year being devoted to lectures—illustrated with the stereopticon—in analysis of the fundamental principles underlying the important creations in ancient and modern plastic arts. The afternoon sessions of the entire course are spent in individual and class criticism of exercises in design which the students are required to execute every week. Through this entire course much stress is laid upon the cultivation of taste and personality, and power to create and to discern.

Weber based his *Essays on Art*, 1916, on lectures that he wrote for the White School in 1914. Though Weber did not teach regularly at the White School after 1918, he maintained a cordial relationship with the school, giving occasional special lectures and serving on its board of advisors in its later years.

As the final component of the program of courses, the 1914 catalogue listed "Criticism of the Work of Students" by Alvin Langdon Coburn, who would (according to the catalogue) also select the prints for the school's annual exhibition. Coburn, a distant cousin of F. Holland Day and a member of the Photo-Secession, was living in England and was an important link to photographers there. Earlier in 1914, as a member of the selecting committee for the 1914 annual exhibition of the Royal Photographic Society, London, Coburn had arranged for twenty-four photographs by eight of White's students, as well as additional photographs by White and by his colleagues, to be shown in a special American section of the exhibition.[35] The 1915 annual exhibition of the Royal Photographic Society, for which Coburn again served on the selecting committee, included the work of some thirteen White students, as well as of White.[36] The 1915 White School catalogue announced that "Coburn, living in London at present, will co-operate in the work of the school as heretofore, and will continue to give his helpful criticism of the students' work."

FRANCES BODE
Printing Room, Clarence H. White
School of Photography, 460 W. 144th
Street, New York, 1922

Even though Coburn was not at hand in New York to critique student work, Clarence White was. Making detailed appraisal of and very specific suggestions on his students' work in his weekly print criticism, he reinforced the importance of composition—which they had been lectured on and drilled in throughout the week—invariably inspiring them to further and higher efforts.

Clarence White had assembled a stellar staff for his school, artists of great experience and talent, all passionately nurturing their students to appreciate and create art. Paul Anderson took the lead in technical matters and provided excellent backup in the philosophy and aesthetics of art photography; Max Weber brought international experience to his analyses of and instruction in composition; Alvin Langdon Coburn, too, provided international perspective and contacts. But it was Clarence White who was the soul and inspiration of the White School, preaching the gospel of art photography.

DESIGN

The emphasis placed on design at the White School cannot be overstated. Max Weber wrote in 1913:

> The photographer's art lies supremely in his choice or disposition of visible objects, as prompted and guided by his intellect and his taste. His mind is his screen. He may shift objects, he may choose his position, he may vary the spaces between movable objects, and finally he may vary the proportion and size of the rectangle bounding the picture or print. After this, he may display rare quality and great skill in the particular art of printing and developing, emphasizing or subduing thereby, tones and contours.[37]

In 1916 Weber declared, "Constant effort is made to help the student in design to bring as much of the abstract into his expression as the photographic means will allow."[38] Students subordinated representation in photographic problems they executed, thus learning to give their photographs better composition. Clarence White emphasized that the photographer "contributes to nature just so much as he has of knowledge of photography, knowledge of composition, knowledge of tone values—he expresses himself that way."[39]

THE "PROJECT METHOD"

The assignment of "problems" was a mainstay of White's teaching. In order to earn course certificates, students had to get instructor approval of completed required projects and problems. Some students had to return a second year to complete requirements for cer-

MILLIE E. HOOPS
Practice Hour (One-and-two-and . . .),
1922

tificates and some never earned them. Technical problems included the production and comparison of the characteristics of a number of processes including oil, hand-sensitized platinum, gum platinum, multiple gum, palladium, cyanotype, and gaslight; and printing from enlarged and paper negatives. A list of suggested compositional problems compiled by instructor Margaret Watkins for a summer school included "One or more figures in relation to line of trees or arbor," "An angular still life!" and "A curved still life!"[40] Another assignment sheet, apparently from the 1920s, included as "subjects" folded white towels, two books, six or more spoons, glasses of milk and water, and as "requirements" form, design relation to rectangle.[41]

Students' photographs testify to the merit of these exercises. Even in the last years of the school, design exercises or "problems" continued to be assigned. According to Margaret Hummel Cohn, a student in 1939–40, "Students were encouraged to choose their own methods and subjects in completing technical assignments."[42]

"A PRACTICAL ART"

The White School was innovative in offering a full-time course in art photography, which promoted its application in amateur, professional, and even commercial work. While the catalogues for White's early summer schools emphasized landscape photography, "for which Seguinland offers an abundance of interesting material," the 1914 catalogue for the first year of the school in New York City, as well as the catalogue for the following year, stated the school's purpose as training its students for the vocation of photographer and referred to photography's role in travel, scientific records, book publishing, and the dissemination of knowledge, before mentioning photography as an art in itself. Topics to be covered by White in his "Art of Photography" course included street and newspaper photography and commercial photography. The school's 1920 and 1922 catalogues noted that the school "treats photography not only as a fine art with an established technique, but also as a practical art, indispensable to modern commerce and industry," and that:

> Calls for technically trained assistants are continually coming in from professional photographers, industrial plants, doctors, schools and colleges, advertising firms, and other sources. Many former students of the school are now established in their own studios, holding important positions with professional photographers, doing home portraiture, producing fine books of photographs, serving as specialists in X-ray and aeroplane work, selling pictures to magazines, professionally employed in department stores and in moving picture studios.

Examples of White alumni who employed photography as a practical art include: Lena G. Towsley, Edith R. Wilson, and Bertha Parker Hall, illustrators of children's books; Cornelia

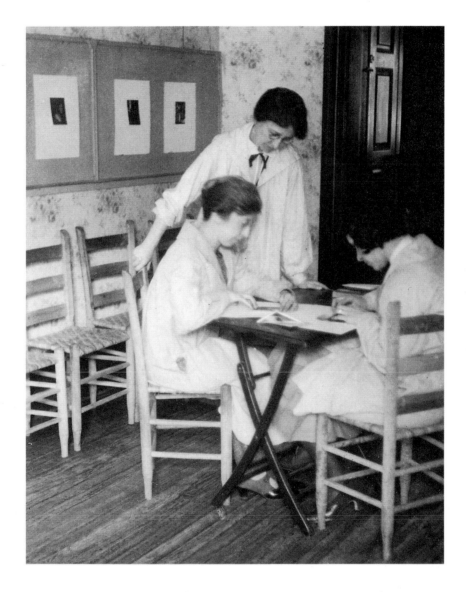

McCoy and Mary B. White, who did X-ray work during World War I; Doris Ulmann, who published books (fig. 15); Laura Gilpin, who also published books, including travel books; Ruth Anderson, Alice Atkinson, and Frances Spalding, photographers for the Hispanic Society, New York; Ira Martin, photographer for the Frick Art Reference Library; Antoinette Hervey, who sold enough photographs to publications to pay for a trip to Europe; Karl Struss and Ralph Steiner, cinematographers; Margaret Watkins, Wynn Richards (fig. 16),

(figure 15)

DORIS ULMANN
"Frank Crowninshield, Editor, Vanity Fair,"
A Portrait Gallery of American Editors *(New York: William Edwin Rudge, 1925), pl. xi.*

Paul Outerbridge Jr., Robert Waida, and Anton Bruehl, who made photographs used in advertisements; and Dorothea Lange for the Farm Security Administration. Early White alumni who served apprenticeships as assistants to established photographers included Margaret Watkins, for portrait photographer Alice Boughton; and Charles Painter, for the photographic illustrator Lejaren à Hiller. Guy Spencer served as assistant to the portrait and fashion photographer Baron Adolph de Meyer.

White believed that students should be taught "fundamentals which are practically the same for all branches of photography." He maintained that training at a school "helps to develop a resourcefulness that seems particularly necessary today in the diversified applications of photography."[43] White advocated the application of artistic principles to a broad spectrum of photography, including professional and commercial, as well as amateur, photography. Notably among his outstanding students, artistic principles were imaginatively and sensitively employed by Paul Outerbridge Jr., Margaret Watkins, and Anton Bruehl, in photography for advertisements; Margaret Bourke-White in industrial photography; and Karl Struss in filming movies.

By 1919 the White School had begun to offer a special ten-week course for the professional portrait photographer, "the object of which will be to give him fresh impetus in his work and to call forth a greater exercise of his art-sense in the service of portraits by photography." The school offered this course throughout the rest of its history.

To cultivate the use of "printing as an artistic craft" in association with photography, the White School offered, at least from 1919 to 1923, a studio course called "Printing and Lettering." In it, Frederic W. Goudy taught typographic design as applied to advertising. Goudy (fig. 17), with whom White had collaborated as far back

RALPH STEINER

After Rehearsal, 1936

as 1911, was the foremost type designer and printer in America; typefaces designed by Goudy continue in wide use today. White himself had a well-established interest in printing.[44] His eldest son, Lewis White, attended Goudy's course at the White School, served as typographer and printer for the school from at least 1920 throughout the rest of its history, and ran his own printing company during this same period.[45]

Some of the practical work produced by alumni and students became prominent in its time. The March 1925 *Exhibition of Photographs by the Students & Alumni of the Clarence H. White School of Photography*, held at the Art Center, New York, included an "Advertising & Commercial Section" consisting of 21 of the 147 works in the exhibition. Among these, *Ide Collars*, by Paul Outerbridge Jr. (see Yochelson, fig. 8), had been published as an advertisement in *Vanity Fair*. Margaret Watkins' *Woodbury's Facial Soap* (p. 158) was presumably related to the photograph reproduced in a Woodbury's Soap advertisement published in the 13 April 1924 *New York Times*. The Advertising & Commercial Section also featured Wynn Richards and Bettie Frear's advertisement for Marshall Field, as well as photographs by Anton Bruehl, Laura Gilpin, Ira W. Martin, and Frances Spalding.

(figure 16)

WYNN RICHARDS
Preparing Yarn for Weaving (National Cotton Council advertisement), 1948

In the later years of the White School, commercial photography became even more conspicuous in its curriculum. From at least 1936 and throughout the rest of its history, the school's catalogues described its class in photographic design and appreciation as including individual and class criticism of photographs submitted as the results of problems in commercial, pictorial, and advertising photography. Princeton University's White Collection includes lists of commercial problem assignments, including story illustration, editorial, fashion, architectural, industrial, and advertising photography.[46] Several students of the later years laid the foundations for their own careers by serving as assistants to established photographers—Edwin Lewis, Dora Maxwell, and George Tichenor for George Platt Lynes; John Roche for Nickolas Muray; Herbert Kratovil and B. Russell Whitaker for Toni Frissell; Eiichi Fukuba and Hans Jorgensen for George Hoyningen-Huene; Hans Jorgensen, Grayson Tewksbury, and Merton Webb for Louise Dahl-Wolfe; and Armin Bomhard and Warren Roll for Wynn Richards.

WYNN RICHARDS

Preparing Yarn for Weaving (National Cotton Council advertisement), 1948

MARGARET WATKINS
Woodbury's Facial Soap
(advertisement), 1924

ROBERT WAIDA
Colgate's Ribbon Dental Cream, 1922

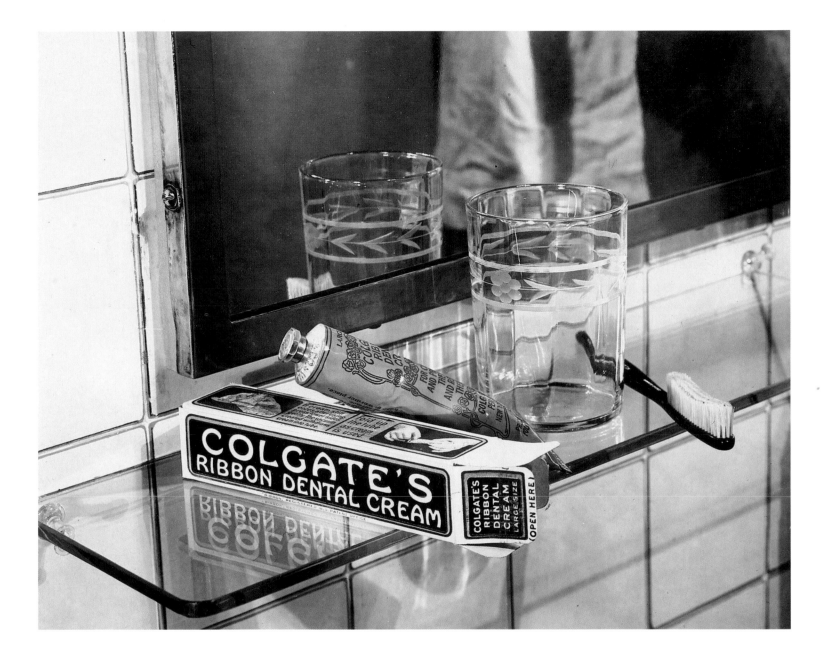

CHANGES IN VENUE

In 1917 both the White School's city and country homes changed (fig. 18). In October 1917 the New York City school moved eight blocks, to the building at 122 East 17th Street known as the Washington Irving House.

After being held in Maine for six years, the summer session was moved to East Canaan, Connecticut in 1916. In 1917 it relocated again to Canaan, Connecticut, only a few miles away, where it continued until Clarence White's death. White School catalogues described both East Canaan and Canaan as situated in the beautiful valley of the Berkshire hills of northern Connecticut, the country furnishing an abundance of photographic opportunity, comprising schools, farms, rolling uplands, streams, rugged mountains, architecture of typically New England character and numerous industries, such as iron furnaces and lime kilns. Paul Anderson's account in 1935 of his teaching with White offered an explanation for the move to Connecticut. He recalled that in 1915

(figure 17)

CLARENCE H. WHITE
Frederic W. Goudy, ca. 1923

White asked me if I would consider a partnership in the school, to which I replied that the coast of Maine was beautiful, but presented overwhelming technical difficulties in the practice of photography; I have seen a man set a rack of negatives on a table between two windows to dry, which it took them slightly more than a week to do. . . . No place for double-coated plates and platinum printing! But at that time I was spending my summers in northern Connecticut, and I agreed to go into partnership in the school if it were moved down there. So it was moved, and turned out to be a very great success, both artistically and financially.[47]

WHITE SCHOOL ALUMNI ASSOCIATION

According to a dissertation on White written by his grandson Maynard Pressley White Jr. using materials collected and arranged by Jane Felix White, "The students at the Maine summer sessions organized their own Seguinland School of Photography Alumni Association by initially surprising the Whites with a dinner in New York during the winter to inform them of this purpose."[48] The earliest "Alumni Association of the Clarence H. White School of Photography" newsletter in the White Collection, Princeton, report-

ed on the "third semi-annual meeting" of the association, 27 November 1916, and referred to the "next" alumni exhibition, as if it had not been the first. The same newsletter noted that "the Alumni voted to extend associate membership to all students of Mr. White, recommended by him," presumably including his students at Columbia and the Brooklyn Institute. In 1917 the alumni association organized two exhibitions of their own photographs, which traveled to various eastern venues, and held further exhibitions during 1920 through 1923 and in 1925.

During the White School summer session in Canaan in 1917, the alumni held a reunion. They issued two publications of selections of their photographs, in 1924 and 1925, each with the title *Camera Pictures*. They did not, however, realize their plans to produce a Clarence H. White memorial book following White's death in 1925.

From at least 1920 on, White School alumni and students enjoyed special lectures—typically offered every Friday evening during the school year—as part of open houses that could also include print criticisms. Prominent among the special lecturers were Alfred Stieglitz and Paul Strand. Lectures by alumni included Paul Outerbridge Jr. on "Living with One's Work" and Doris Ulmann on publishing her most recent book of photographs, both given in 1925. Among many others, lectures were given by Edward Steichen at least from 1923 and throughout the rest of the history of the school (Steichen was a member of the school's board of advisors from at least 1933), the dancer Bird Larson on rhythmic expression in 1923, Francis Bruguière in 1924, Arnold

(figure 18)

EDWARD R. DICKSON (top)
ELEANOR C. ERVING (bottom)
Photo=Graphic Art, *vol. 3, no. 2*
(October 1917): inside front cover

Genthe in 1925, and Roy Stryker in 1941. Margaret Watkins's contact with Pierce Johnson, art director for the advertising firm J. Walter Thompson Co., when he gave a special lecture at the school in February 1924, resulted in several valuable commissions for her.[49]

PICTORIAL PHOTOGRAPHERS OF AMERICA

In 1917, the same year that the White School relocated to Canaan, Connecticut, and to the Washington Irving House in New York City, and that the White School alumni association was actively arranging exhibitions, another organization with which Clarence White was closely involved began its long history. This was the Pictorial Photographers

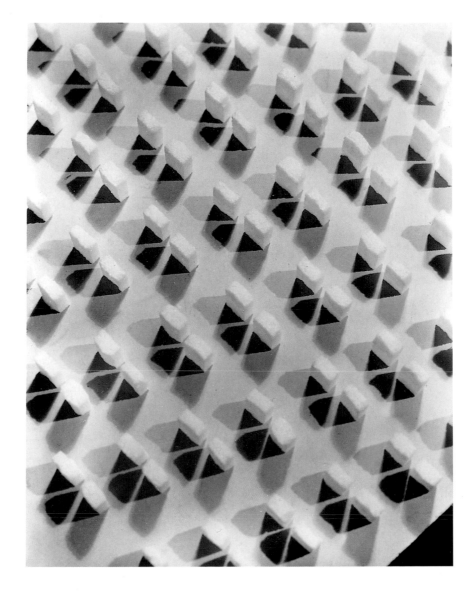

MARGARET WATKINS

Design for Marble Floor,
"Blythswood," Glasgow, 1937

ESTELLE WOLF

Polish Pavilion, New York World's Fair,
1939

167

of America (PPA), a national group with open membership, whose objectives of exhibiting and promoting pictorial photography echoed those of the White School.[50] In the 1917–18 traveling exhibition described as introducing the PPA to the public, White School alumni counted for at least thirty-one of the fifty-seven exhibitors.[51] White was president of the PPA from 1917 to 1921 and, during his lifetime, the PPA's annual meeting was frequently if not always held in conjunction with the White School summer session in Connecticut.

STUDENTS BECOME TEACHERS

Overall, former students made up the majority of White School instructors. Karl Struss served as the precursor of these students-turned-teachers. Struss had studied with White at Columbia from 1908 to 1912 and taught photography classes at Columbia in the summer of 1912 and at the Brooklyn Institute of Arts and Sciences in the fall of 1916.

Margaret Watkins, a White student beginning about 1914 and a staff member from about 1919 until 1925, was remembered by her student Ralph Steiner as the one who checked off technical problems—tough but helpful.[52] Margaret Bourke-White, a Columbia student in 1921–22, some years later wished for Watkins's "old-time, much-appreciated onceover of my work."[53] Bernard Horne, a White School student in 1915–16, took Paul Anderson's place and taught "Technique of Photography" at the school from 1918 to 1928, continuing to teach a wide variety of photographic print processes.

Charles J. Martin was White's student at Teachers College from 1916 to 1918 while earning a B.S. degree. Martin was on the White School staff from about 1919 to 1933, replacing Max Weber in teaching art appreciation and design. In 1919 John Heins studied with White at Teachers College, which awarded him an M.A. degree in 1939; Heins taught design at the White School from 1920 until it closed in 1942.

Arthur Chapman, several times a White student between 1910 and 1917, ran a White School summer session in New York City in 1921 with former White student Joseph Mason. Anton Bruehl, a White student ca. 1923, was a member of the school staff from ca. 1924 to 1926 and served on its board of advisors from at least 1933.

Robert Waida, a White School student in 1921–22, taught "Studio Practice" from 1925 to 1932. Waida's gifts as a teacher were confirmed by Victor Keppler, who was not a White School student but served as Waida's assistant: "Waida was both a professional and a patient man, for he explained not only what he was doing but why. By the end of our relationship, I had learned how to build a still life—one of the most exacting techniques in the repertoire of the complete photographer. . . . He could teach these things."[54]

Alfred Cohn, White School class of 1918, taught school summer sessions held in Woodstock, New York, from 1931 to 1933, and taught at the school in New York City full time from at least 1940 until it closed in 1942. In 1948 Cohn founded the Arizona School of Photography, which perpetuated White's teaching principles.

(figure 19)

UNIDENTIFIED
PHOTOGRAPHER
The Bulletin of the Alumni,
Clarence H. White School of
Photography, Housewarming
Number (December 1920): cover.

THE GOLDEN YEARS: 460 WEST 144TH STREET

A great change for the school came in 1920 when it moved to 460 West 144th Street (fig. 19). Since the Washington Irving House would not be available for use by the school following the 1919–20 school year, the school advisory board decided to sell stock in the Clarence H. White Realty Corporation, formed specifically to acquire a building to rent to the school for its use.[55] The purchase of stock was presented to alumni as "an opportunity to show loyalty, to give help at a critical time, to share in an enterprise that is worth while."[56]

The plan for the school—with more space, more staff, and evening courses—was to take on more pupils than it had been able to serve in the Washington Irving House. The alumni bulletin reported on many solo alumni exhibitions in the new exhibition room. The Whites also lived at the new location, which left White farther from the Brooklyn Institute but closer to Columbia University. In fact, his Teachers College photography classes actually met at 460 West 144th Street.

LATER SUMMER SCHOOLS

In 1921 the White School offered summer sessions in both New York City and Canaan, Connecticut. Canaan continued as the home of the school's summer sessions until White's death in 1925. After a hiatus, Woodstock, New York, hosted White School summer sessions from 1931 to 1933. From 1934 on, they were offered only in New York City.[57]

White mentioned the possibility of traveling photography classes as early as 1913.[58] Jane White remembered that many times her husband "had been approached by enthusiasts who were desirous that he should conduct such a class in England, or

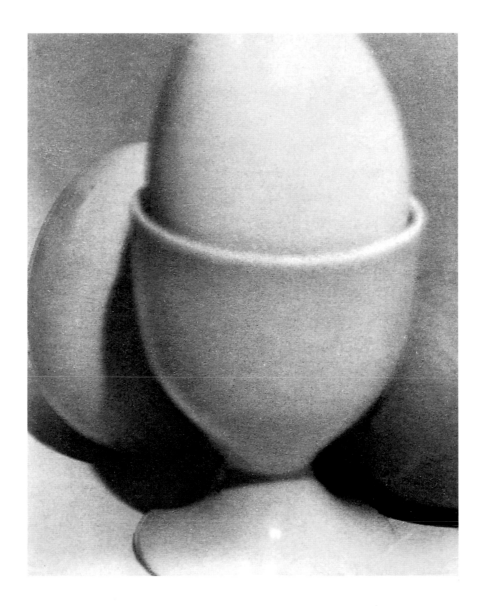

certain parts of Europe. Much traveled routes[,] however, did not seem to interest him."[59] White's only such class, reportedly of six students, in the summer of 1925 traveled to Mexico, where White died of an aortic aneurysm.[60]

THE ART CENTER

Even as the Clarence H. White Realty Corporation was arranging for a new home for the White School, White was serving as a member of the committee that brought the Art Center into being. The Art Center was a union of groups, the Pictorial Photographers of America among them, that promoted the decorative crafts and the industrial and graphic arts of America. The PPA held its monthly meetings at the Center's central location at 65–67 East 56th Street, which opened in October 1921. These meetings often included special lectures, not unlike the Friday evening lectures that continued at the White School.

The Art Center, perhaps more significantly, also provided centrally located galleries for exhibitions, including exhibitions of photographs by White and his students and alumni, many of whom were active in the PPA. *The Bulletin of the Alumni, Clarence H. White School of Photography*, November 1921, reported that White School alumni accounted for fifty of the eighty-three exhibitors in the first exhibition of the PPA at the Art Center, held that month. Anton Bruehl's decision to devote himself to photography as a result of seeing such an exhibition in 1923 is a dramatic example of the potential influence of these exhibitions.[61] Clarence White's photographs were shown at the Art Center in the exhibitions *Stowaways and Ships*, 9–21 February 1925, and the *Memorial Exhibition of the Work of Clarence H. White*, 14–30 April 1926. The Art Center hosted an *Exhibition of Photographs by the Students & Alumni of the Clarence H. White School of Photography*, 16–21 March 1925. From 1923 to 1931, the Art Center presented solo exhibitions of the work of at least sixteen White School alumni. More than half of these were held in 1924 and 1925, during the last year and a half of Clarence White's life. The White students so honored were Allie Bramberg Bode, Anton Bruehl, Laura Gilpin, Eugene Henry, Antoinette B. Hervey, Bernard S. Horne, Dr. Charles Jaeger, Ira W. Martin, Henry Hoyt Moore, Paul Outerbridge Jr., Joseph Petrocelli, Stella F. Simon, Doris Ulmann, Robert Waida, Margaret Watkins, and Delight Weston.[62]

In 1921, with the Art Center launched, White stepped down from the presidency of the Pictorial Photographers of America. The PPA Bulletin reported that White did so "not because of his desire to be relieved of the work, but because of his feeling that the

organization would be benefited by a change."[63] The responsibilities of the larger premises and additional students at the White School's new West 144th Street home did prompt White to stop teaching at the Brooklyn Institute of Arts and Sciences in 1922.[64]

"THIS PROBLEM OF FINANCES"

Though a gifted and influential teacher, White did not have the capacity for systematizing his work to make it easy to manage—something he had admitted in a reference to his instruction at Teachers College.[65] His inability to be business oriented—even though he taught photography as "a practical art"—brought the school to a crossroads. Walter L. Hervey, in his capacity as secretary-treasurer of the Clarence H. White Realty Corporation, wrote to its board of directors in September 1922 to state that he had determined that the White School could not be a paying proposition. To protect the interests of the stockholders, Hervey said, the building should be sold. He noted that the plan for the school in its new West 144th Street location was to accommodate fifty students.

> It was felt that 50 regular students would pay all expenses and leave a reasonable income for Mr. White, but Mr. White has since found that the number of students he can handle effectively is considerably less than his original estimate. In fact, he has stated that the limit was reached during the last school year. But the accounts of the school during the last school year show an income of some $9,000 offset by expenses of an equal amount, not including any remuneration to Mr. White himself.[66]

Indeed, Hervey noted that the school had also been negligent in paying the Realty Corporation the rent due it. Tuition figures for the school suggest the "limit" of students may have been no more than approximately twenty-five.[67] The tuition fee charged for the basic course at the White School had climbed from $75 per half year in 1914 to $125 in 1917. From about 1920 and throughout the rest of the school's history, the tuition charged for the basic course remained at $150 per half year.

Walter Hervey had been a supporter of the White School from at least 1915, a member of its advisory board, and a lecturer at the school. His wife, Antoinette B. Hervey, was an alumna. The Herveys considered themselves ardent supporters of White and his school. However, they were not part of the group that White described as "particularly friendly toward the school," a group that pushed for the White School's continued residence on West 144th Street.[68]

A majority vote of the stockholders ratified this alternative plan at a meeting on 27 November 1922. White explained his plan:

> To continue the school along the lines on which I conducted it before moving uptown,

namely to restrict the number of pupils to a comparatively small group instead of attempting to handle 50 pupils. The experience of the last two years has shown that the overhead expenses for the instruction of 50 pupils are much higher proportionately than the expense for the instruction of a smaller number of pupils. With not more than 10 to 15 pupils in the school I will have time for my own work which will be a source of income to me in addition to the tuition fees of the pupils. An additional source of revenue to me will be the rental of a studio in the building to Mr. [Charles J.] Martin, one of our instructors.[69]

While enrollment limits are not otherwise known to have been given in White School catalogues, an announcement of the 1923–24 school year began "Fifteen applicants will be accepted to form the class."

A "CULTURAL RESOURCE"

By all available evidence, Clarence H. White was sincerely motivated by potential good to his students and to anyone else he could influence. His great goal was to stimulate their appreciation of art and, thereby, their greater appreciation of life, with photography as a means to this end.[70] In April 1901 White had written to Alfred Stieglitz: "I have made up my mind that art in photography will be my life work and am preparing to live a very simple life with my little family to carry this out."[71] While teaching photography may have brought in barely enough money to support his family, to Clarence White, financial reward was subordinate to the cultural influence he had on his students. Jane White noted her husband's philosophy that while others are "breaking their necks to earn money with which to buy their pleasure, I do not need to, for I get my pleasure in my work, and am just that far ahead of them!"[72] Clarence White affirmed "our standard [is] to plant the 'seed of enthusiasm' above any thought of profit in our School."[73] According to one who knew him well, White "was always at odds with materialism, his sense of values being confined to the spiritual and humanitarian."[74]

White's satisfaction with his success in achieving his goal was reflected in an announcement for the 1923–24 school year:

> The studies and associations of this school have yielded values for which there is no material measure. Men and women have found themselves, worked out a better adjustment to life, and discovered new sources of interest and happiness. Photography as it is taught in the Clarence H. White School becomes a financial or cultural resource—or both.

The ongoing support and praise of White by his students testify to their appreciation of the cultural resources he nurtured.

A Natural, Subtle Teacher

As has been noted, Jane White, Ema Spencer, and Alfred Stieglitz all attested that Clarence H. White was a natural teacher. An important aspect of his teaching was his limiting the number of his students to only about fifteen, even when facilities could accommodate more. As was often observed, White fostered the individuality of the work of his students, advocating the achievement of their individual expression as a primary function of art photography.

Numerous comments by students of White point to the subtlety of his teaching. As a student in the Maine summer class of 1910, Arthur Chapman noticed that, as for "those who can, do; those who cannot, teach . . . it holds good with Mr. White. He does not teach. His criticisms and comments merely set the students mor[e] diligently at work upon their several salvations in their several ways—not by main strength, either, but with self-confidence."[75] John Wallace Gillies, a photographer and writer on photography in White's circle, commented in 1915:

> A teacher of repute, Mr. White will not dwell upon how he does it—a curious anomaly, for he has manufactured many of photography's best workers. You must go to him to learn, and yet he would not tell you, for he wants you to do it for yourself, instead of living in an atmosphere which is not your own. In the air around him you will feel the impulse to make pictures. I speak of Mr. White as an amateur, and though he derives his living from photography, he is one of the greatest amateurs.[76]

Elsewhere, Gillies defined "amateur" as "any person who does a thing for the sheer love of doing it and receives no financial return for the performance."[77] Dorothea Lange, a White student at Teachers College during the teens, said during an interview in 1968:

> [White was] a very extraordinary teacher. Why he was extraordinary has puzzled me ever since because he didn't do anything. . . . He would and did accept everything. He was most uncritical. He always saw the print in relation to the person. . . . But the point is that he gave everyone some feeling of encouragement in some peculiar way. You walked into that dreary room knowing that something was going to happen. Now what happened I don't know, but you never forgot it. I can hear his voice still.
>
> That man was a good teacher, a great teacher . . . he encouraged along a little bit, nudged here and there. . . . I don't know people whose work looks like Clarence White's, which, of course, is a great recommendation to him as a teacher, validates what I said, that a student's work didn't look like his. But he touched lives.[78]

Anton Bruehl, one of White's last pupils, remembered:
He showed each of us a way to think for ourselves. He let each of us follow our own desires. Very little pressure was exerted on us as students. Rather, his approach was to guide us to do it well, follow our inclinations and imaginations, and to be sincere! It was mainly by association that you received what you learned from Clarence White.[79]

KENNETH A. LINN

Flower Abstract (photogram), 1929

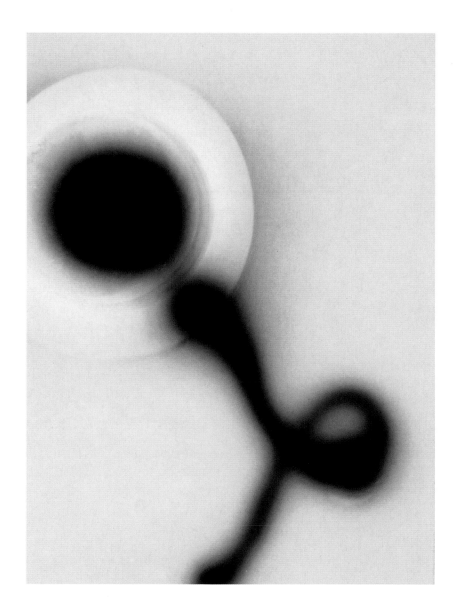

Edward R. Dickson, in an article in *Photo-Era* (January 1913) on White's teaching, described White as ever ready "to proffer desired criticism so constructive in tendency as to bring out the good points, rather than to direct attention to faults too obvious for censure." In addition, Dickson observed:

> Since Mr. White encourages individual attitude in photography, he purposely avoids comparing the work of one student with that of another, a policy to which he adheres throughout the entire year. Not only does he teach the fundamentals . . . but the need of finding a given space and form for expressing that which the student desires; for one's art must be individual feeling and expression, not simply representation.[80]

James N. Giridlian, in his capacity as officer in charge of photographic instruction in the U.S. Navy and the Marine Corps, wrote to White in 1918. Giridlian, who had been White's student from about 1913 to 1916, evaluated what makes a good photographer. He stated:

> While in your school I was taught to use my head instead of making myself a slave to the pet processes of this and that instructor. I find that while most photographers are made by having their individuality suppressed, you are turning out much better photographers, technically and otherwise, by developing what little individuality they might have.[81]

White student Henry Hoyt Moore published in *The Outlook*, whose illustration and printing departments he managed, "samples of remembered criticisms" given by White at his summer school in 1916. They were also quoted in the 1922 catalogue for the White summer school:

> "There should be something of interest in every part of your print"; "That obtrusive high light takes something away from what you are really photographing, and should be sunned down"; "That is very nice; the interest follows pleasantly from the arm to the head, then to the overhanging bough, and that leads us back again"; "The foreground is mushy; you must learn to focus"; "That is very good indeed; there is in it a nice quality of light and shade"; "The figure would be better if placed a little higher on the plate"; "Now you need an accent of light here; watch me put in a high-light"—and the lecturer puts a small piece of white paper on the proof, to its manifest improvement; "That is so good that I would like to see it done over again."[82]

Moore continued, "No one is ever offended by this genial teacher. He is so manifestly anxious for the improvement of the learner that the victim of his severest criticism gets some consolation out of it and resolves at once to try it again, and this time make a picture worth while."

> Marie Riggins Higbee Avery, a 1922 summer school student, observed:
> The meat of Clarence White's criticism was not concerned with technique but with composition and design, of which he was a master. . . . Good spacing, fine balance, the proper amount of detail to enrich the areas, fine distribution of values, these were the

MARGARET WATKINS

*Verna and Teacup (Cutex
advertisement), 1924*

essentials demanded of each print. . . . Whatever effort was back of each print he sensed, and measured out his criticism in proportion. With casual work he was sharp or ignored it altogether. With sincere effort he was encouraging in spite of failures. Within a few days after our arrival he had taken the measure of our capacities and he relentlessly held us to maximum production, according to our individual abilities.[83]

Avery also noted:

We were taught a rigid type of selectivity in the Canaan school, which did not condone making an exposure of slight merit at the end of a futile search, in order to have something to show for the effort. . . . Coming to a criticism empty handed did not evoke any censure from Clarence White. "Too many exposures need never have been made," he often said.

References to the self-confidence White instilled are telling. Walter Hervey and Laura Gilpin referred to White's commentary on his students' work as "sympathetic yet searching criticisms that faithfully showed them how weak they were yet always somehow made them courageous and strong."[84] Jane White observed of her husband: "Since his faith in things to which he gave his support was express[ed] with such a buoyant spirit, it inspired faith in others, and created real joy in participation."[85] Marie Riggins Higbee Avery summarized what White had done for his students: "The rigor of our training, together with an indominable [sic] spirit fostered in each of us, a result of Clarence White's teaching, was to carry a few of the least promising of the group to places of high honor in the photographic world."[86]

THE WHITE SCHOOL AFTER WHITE'S DEATH

In some ways, the philosophy of the Clarence H. White School of Photography remained unchanged after White's death in 1925. *The Camera*, in July 1933, quoted the comments of an unidentified visitor to a public exhibition of the work of the school's 1932–33 students: "The outstanding characteristic of the whole affair was the absence of 'teacher dominance' for the prints certainly show originality and freedom of expression." *The Camera* added: "That the White School is doing a great work in developing talent rather than attempting to mold it, is quite evident in the many original subjects exhibited."

However, following White's death, Alfred Stieglitz predicted to the Austrian photographer Heinrich Kühn: "The school that he founded will not be able to exist without him. He was the school—That is his personality which was truly very nice—nothing harsh about it like we have."[87] Teachers College, in fact, did not continue to offer courses in art photography following White's death. According to the circa 1939 *Clarence H. White School of Photography, A Memorial to Its Founder:*

JULIA MARSHALL
Hershey's (advertisement),
1922/1927

The personality of Mr. White had been such an important factor in the school, that, upon first thought, it seemed that the institution could not survive without him; but many of his co-workers and students had such faith in the future of the work, that they urged the continuation of the school as the most fitting memorial to his life and accomplishments in photography. So many felt that this would be his wish, that Mrs. White was finally persuaded to carry on the work, with the loyal and able assistance of those who had for years worked side by side with Clarence White in his development of the school.

Jane White, whose assumption of her husband's position as director was recorded in the 1925 school catalogue, was neither a photography teacher nor a photographer. Nonetheless, her correspondence shows that she unequivocally accepted the responsibility of the White School students' education. For example, during her first year as director, she would not jeopardize school standards to save money. This possibility arose when Anton Bruehl left his position as instructor of studio practice and evening courses at the school to devote more time to other work. Even though longtime instructor Bernard Horne thought that Bruehl's position did not need to be filled, Mrs. White declared that she must carry out her contract with her students. To do so, she hired Robert Waida as lab director.[88] Furthermore, she recorded, "I am planning to make many improvements in equipment & general working facilities, & do feel things are promising. C.[larence] Jr. is enthusiastic & can help in many ways."[89] Mrs. White was ready to consider new courses, such as one devoted to advertising photography,[90] although it was not finally offered until many years later. On 4 January 1928 she noted, "Yesterday our school re-opened—& I am up early & late too, for I am chief everything."[91]

Jane White hoped that her youngest son, Clarence H. White Jr. (1907–1978), would eventually join her in the administration of the school.[92] According to his resumés, he was a freelance photographer from 1925, a student at the White School 1926–27, and an assistant instructor at the school from June 1927 to January 1928. Due to illness, he did not work from September 1929 to October 1931, when he rejoined the school staff as assistant director and also taught photographic technique and practice. He was director of the school by 1939.[93] Jane White also continued as director of the school until 1940, when she became director emeritus.

EXPANSION OF THE WHITE SCHOOL

Jane White and Clarence White Jr. both wished to increase enrollment at the school, not sharing Clarence Sr.'s preference for small classes. Indeed, Jane White had advocated accepting more students during her husband's lifetime, writing early in 1917: "Our

EDITH WINIFRED TAIT

Study of a Hand, 1926

school is so full that Clarence feels he has reached its limit as to capacity, & more are wanting to come, & I say let them. It is just as easy to lecture to a room full, as few: the problem is the dark-room & printing room."[94] Along with the loss of the personality of Clarence Sr., the school's expansion represented another major change for the White School following its founder's death. According to *Clarence H. White School of Photography, A Memorial to Its Founder,* Clarence White Jr.'s aim had been

> . . . constantly to improve and expand the curriculum, and thereby develop the school as a living memorial to its founder.

> For the first two years the effect of the new curriculum on the enrollment was not apparent, but since 1934 the rise has been both definite and continuous. From about twenty students in 1922 enrollment increased year by year to one hundred and six students in 1939, with income rising from $5,310.00 to $15,812.00 in the same period.

By the 1934–35 school year, the increased number of students was made up of a majority of men, reversing the ratio of women to men that had prevailed among the students during Clarence White Sr.'s lifetime.

School catalogues following the death of Clarence Sr. ceased to mention cultivation of taste and personality, though instruction in art appreciation continued to be included as a segment of every course. From about 1933, however, course descriptions no longer reflected the integration of art and technique that was once a hallmark of the school. Photographic technique had apparently superseded design as the school's emphasis.

CLARENCE·H·WHITE SCHOOL OF PHOTOGRAPHY

32 WEST·74 STREET·NEW YORK·N.Y.

(figure 20)

UNIDENTIFIED
PHOTOGRAPHER
Clarence H. White School of Photography, A Memorial to Its Founder, ca. 1939, cover.

THE END OF THE SCHOOL: 32 WEST 74TH STREET

In 1940 the school moved to larger premises, more centrally located at 32 West 74th Street (fig. 20). At the celebratory housewarming for the school's new home, photographer Ansel Adams spoke of "the predominant force the White School had always been and was in the world of photographic education."[95]

The school introduced a class in photojournalism, taught by *Life* photographer Eliot Elisofon, as well as a course in motion picture technique and practice. It reintroduced a course in advertising and graphic problems related to photographs (Frederic W. Goudy had taught the predecessor to this course at the school from about 1919 to 1923).

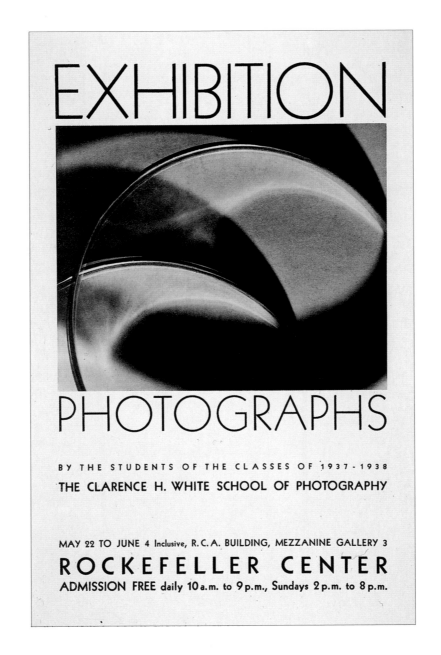

The years of World War II turned out to be an unfortunate time for the school's expansion, however. Despite efforts to find financial support to meet the school's obligations, it closed in 1942. In its final days the school offered its staff photographs by Clarence White Sr. in lieu of salary it could not afford to pay.[96]

Jane Felix White outlived the Clarence H. White School of Photography by less than a year. Clarence H. White Jr., after serving as a photographer and teaching photography for the U.S. Navy, practiced and taught photography in Maine from 1946 to 1949. From 1949 until his retirement in 1972, he was a faculty member at Ohio University, Athens, where he served for most of that time as head of the photography department.[97]

THE LEGACY OF CLARENCE H. WHITE

The influence of Clarence H. White extended throughout a wide network, starting with his friends, students, and—through exhibitions and the Pictorial Photographers of America—art photographers he may never have met. As a photographer and a teacher, White unquestionably had a tremendous impact, inspiring lives and art alike. One of his students, Stella Simon, spoke for most: "Anyone who came under his influence never got over it."[98] White instilled in his students the confidence to strive for improvement in their work. Many of them, indeed, produced highly successful photographs, notably embodying the thoughtful expression and picture composition that White stressed. Such work is the legacy of Clarence H. White and his teaching.

1 Letter, Clarence H. White to Laura Gilpin, 8 November 1922, Gilpin Papers.

2 Jane Felix White, untitled, unpublished note on Clarence H. White, typescript, 1942, White Collection, Princeton.

3 Announcement of Clarence H. White School of Photography Friday evening lectures and demonstrations, ca. 1923; Lorado Taft, "Clarence H. White and the Newark (Ohio) Camera Club," *Brush and Pencil*, vol. 3, no. 2 (November 1898): 105. White would have heard Beck speak on composition in photography at both the 1896 and 1897 conventions of the Photographers' Association of Ohio, both held in Columbus ("The Photographers' Association of Ohio," *Photographic Times*, vol. 29, no. 10 [October 1897]: 493–95).

4 Stieglitz Archive.

5 Clarence H. White, "The Progress of Pictorial Photography, An Interview with Henry Hoyt Moore," in *Annual Report of the Pictorial Photographers of America* (New York: Pictorial Photographers of America, 1918), 8.

6 The importance to Clarence White of interchange with his fellow Photo-Secessionists is attested to by Jane Felix White ("Photographer's Holiday," 10).

7 Letter, Clarence H. White to F. Holland Day, 5 January 1907, Norwood.

8 The extension courses taught by Clarence White were held at Teachers College, Columbia University. Columbia University itself, however, and not Teachers College, administered the extension courses. White also taught art photography for Columbia University during the summer of 1911.

9 *School of Industrial Arts, Teachers College, Columbia University, Day and Evening Courses in Art Photography*, ca. 1911, Stephen White Collection, Los Angeles.

10 Alfred Stieglitz, "Clarence H. White Becomes A Teacher 1907," conversation with Dorothy Norman (sometime during the years 1927 to 1946), unpublished manuscript, collection of Dorothy Norman, excerpts transcribed by Peter C. Bunnell.

11 Jane Felix White, unpublished note on Clarence H. White, typescript, 1942, White Collection, Princeton. This note, like the one in "Society News" (*American Photography*, vol. 1, no. 2 [August 1907]: 110), mentioned the involvement of Stieglitz but not of Dow.

12 Marks, "Peaceful Warrior," 168 (see p. 116, note 2).

13 Marie Riggins (Higbee Avery), "Modern Pictorial Photography and The Measure of Its Art" (Ph.D. diss., Western Reserve University, 1943), 3. Riggins studied at Teachers College ca. 1919–24.

14 Margaret Bourke-White, *Portrait of Myself* (New York: Simon and Schuster, 1963), 29.

15 *School of Industrial Arts* (note 9 above).

16 Letter, Clarence H. White to F. Holland Day, 19 June 1907, Norwood.

17 Letter, Clarence H. White to F. Holland Day, 11 February 1908, Norwood.

18 Clarence H. White, quoted in John Wallace Gillies, *Principles of Pictorial Photography* (New York: Falk Publishing Company, Inc., 1923), 25.

19 *Columbia University Bulletin of Information Announcement of Extension Teaching, 1908–1909* (New York: Columbia University, 1908): 46; *Columbia University Bulletin of Information Announcement of Extension Teaching, 1909–1910* (New York: Columbia University, 1909): 39.

20 *The Year Book of The Brooklyn Institute of Arts and Sciences* (Brooklyn: Brooklyn Institute of Arts and Sciences, 1894–1903); *The Brooklyn Institute of Arts and Sciences Prospectus* (Brooklyn: Brooklyn Institute of Arts and Sciences, 1894–1903).

21 *The Twenty-first Year Book of the Brooklyn Institute of Arts and Sciences, 1908–1909* (Brooklyn: The Brooklyn Institute of Arts and Sciences, 1909): 198.

22 *Bulletin of The Brooklyn Institute of Arts and Sciences*, vol. 3, no. 5 (9 October 1909): 110.

23 "Photographer's Holiday," 45.

24 "History of the School," typescript carbon, ca. 1940, White Collection, Princeton. According to *Memorial*, the school was "founded in 1910 . . . for a selected group who desired his personal guidance. The success of this venture led to the establishment of the school in New York City in 1914."

25 Letter, Anne Brigman to [Alfred] Stieglitz, 9 July 1910, Stieglitz Archive; "Article by Arthur Chapman, student of Clarence. Maine. 1910," typescript, White Collection, Princeton.

26 Although the numbering of White summer schools suggests that the schools were held yearly from 1910 on, 1911 may be an exception. This author has not found a catalogue for a White summer school held in Maine that year, while Columbia University did offer a summer course in photography taught by White, 5 July–16 August 1911.

27 "Photographer's Holiday," 99.

28 Letter, Clarence H. White to Alvin Langdon Coburn, 20 July 1913, George Eastman House.

29 Letter, Jane Felix White to Laura Gilpin, 6 February 1927, Gilpin Papers; letter, Jane Felix White to F. Holland Day, 11 February 1930, Norwood.

30 Advertisements in *Platinum Print* (vol. 1, no. 6 [November 1914]: ii[?]; vol. 2, no. 1 [1915]: i) and an editorial reference in *Platinum Print* (vol. 1, no. 6 [November 1914]: 14), include "Modern." "Modern" was not included in the name of the school in an advertisement run in *Platinum Print*, vol. 2, no. 2 (1915): i.

31 *A Professional Course for the Professional Worker in the Clarence H. White School of Photography*, 1919.

32 Paul L. Anderson, "Where Are We to Get Our Pictorialists?" *Platinum Print*, vol. 1, no. 4 (May 1914): 5.

33 Paul L. Anderson, "The Education of the Photographic Artist," *Photo-Era*, vol. 35, no. 6 (December 1915): 272.

34 "The Reminiscences of Max Weber," interviewed by Carol S. Gruber, Oral History Research Office, Columbia University, 1958, 277–78.

35 Letter, Alvin Langdon Coburn to Max Weber, 29 April 1914, Joy Weber Collection; "The Royal Photographic Society of Great Britain. . . . Fifty-Ninth Annual Exhibition, 1914," *The Photographic Journal*, vol. 54, Supplement (August 1914).

36 "The Royal Photographic Society of Great Britain. . . . Sixtieth Annual Exhibition, 1915," *The Photographic Journal*, vol. 55, Supplement (August 1915).

37 Max Weber, "The Filling of Space," *Platinum Print*, vol. 1, no. 2 (December 1913): 6.

38 M. W. [Max Weber], "Design," *Photo=Graphic Art*, vol. 3, no. 1 (June 1916): 8.

39 White, "Progress of Pictorial Photography" (note 5 above), 14.

40 [Joseph] Mulholland Archive of materials collected by Margaret Watkins, Glasgow, Scotland.

41 White Collection, Princeton.

42 Letter, Margaret H. Cohn and Jeremy Stowall to Kathleen A. Erwin, 30 December 1993, Coville Collection.

43 Clarence H. White, "Photography as a Profession for Women," *News-Bulletin of the Bureau of Vocational Information*, vol. 2, no. 7 (1 April 1924): 54–55 (reprinted in *American Photography*, vol. 18, no. 7 [July 1924]: 432, and quoted in White School catalogues at least from 1936).

44 "Little Life Stories of Live Men Known to the Printers of America, Clarence H. White, Artist Photographer," *The American Printer*, vol. 74, no. 2 (5 February 1922): 31.

45 Jane Felix White, untitled typescript, undated, White Collection, Princeton.

46 "All Students Are Requested to Photograph and Make Prints as Follows:" undated; "Assignments for Course #11 Design Class," 1941; "Course 18 Advanced," undated, ca. 1936–42; "Design—Miss Riley," undated, ca. 1939–42.

47 Paul L. Anderson, "Some Pictorial History," *American Photography*, vol. 29, no. 4 (April 1935): 204, 206. This writer has not seen any other contemporary reference to a partnership between White and Anderson.

48 M. P. White 1975, 179–80, without date or source given.

49 "Clarence H. White School of Photography, List of Friday Evening Lectures, 1923–24," annotated, mimeographed, Mulholland Archive.

50 The PPA held its first regular monthly meeting in February 1917 (*Pictorial Photographers of America 1917* [New York: Pictorial Photographers of America, 1918], 6, 10).

51 Edward R. Dickson, "Pictorial Photographers of America, Its Work and Its Aims," *Photo=Graphic Art*, vol. 3, no. 2 (October 1917): 18; Detroit Museum of Art, "Sculpture by Mrs. Gertrude Vanderbilt Whitney and Pictorial Photographs by American Artists," 1918.

52 Ralph Steiner, "An Interview with Ralph Steiner," in *A Collective Vision: Clarence H. White and His Students*, ed. Lucinda Barnes (Long Beach: University Art Museum, California State University, 1985), 28.

53 Letter, Margaret Bourke-White to Margaret Watkins [December 1927], Mulholland Archive.

54 Victor Keppler, *Man + Camera* (New York: Amphoto, 1970), 30, 31.

55 Letter, Committee of the Advisory Board of the Clarence H. White School of Photography to the Alumni and Other Friends of the Clarence H. White School of Photography, 5 April 1920, Norwood and Gilpin Papers.

56 *The Bulletin of the Alumni, Clarence H. White School of Photography*, June 1921.

57 The 1933 full-year school catalogue stated that the 1934 summer session would be held in Woodstock, but the 1934 New York City summer school catalogue noted: "This course replaces the six weeks course formerly held in Woodstock, N.Y."

58 Letter, Clarence H. White to Alvin Langdon Coburn, 20 July 1913, George Eastman House.

59 "Photographer's Holiday," 126.

60 Lillian Sabine, "Mrs. Stella F. Simon, New York City," *Abel's Photographic Weekly*, vol. 50, no. 1293 (1 October 1932): 235; M. P. White 1975, 240–43.

61 "The Brothers Bruehl," *U.S. Camera*, vol. 1, no. 3 (March–April 1939): 47. Mildred Stagg, in "Anton Bruehl" (*Modern Photography*, vol. 15, no. 9 [September 1951]: 29), gave an alternative version, which did not name a venue for the influential exhibition of pictures "by students at the Clarence White School."

62 Watkins, December 1923; Gilpin, 10 January to 6 February 1924; Henry, 5–29 February 1924; Outerbridge, 5–31 March 1924; Martin, 8 April – 6 May 1924; Moore, 6–31 May 1924; Petrocelli, 3–29 November 1924; Hervey, 12–24 January 1925; Jaeger, 4–31 May 1925; Weston, 5–30 January 1926; Horne, 1–31 March 1926; Bramberg Bode, May 1926; Ulmann, 1–27 November 1926; Bruehl, December 1926; Waida, 1–28 February 1927; Martin, 17–29 October 1927; Simon, 19–31 January 1931 (*Art Center Bulletin*, vols. 2–9 [January 1924 to January 1931]).

63 "The October Meeting," The Bulletin (October 1921), White Collection, Princeton.

64 Previously, 1921 has consistently been given as the date of White's resignation from teaching at the Brooklyn Institute, presumably based on "Notes for Newark Advocate," typescript, undated (sometime during the years 1921 to 1925), White Collection, Princeton, which includes "Appointed lecturer in Brooklyn Institute of Arts & Sciences, 1908. Resigned 1921." However, not only was the carbon copy of White's resignation letter, in the White Collection, Princeton, dated 1 May 1922, but he was also listed as the teacher of the artistic photography course in *The Brooklyn Institute of Arts and Sciences . . . Prospectus 1921–1922* (Brooklyn: Brooklyn Institute of Arts and Sciences, 1921), 83–84, and the *Bulletin of the Brooklyn Institute of Arts and Sciences* (vol. 26, no. 1 [10 September 1921]: 15); and the *Exhibition of Prints, by Clarence H. White's class in Artistic Photography*, 24–28 April 1922, was announced in the *Bulletin of the Brooklyn Institute of Arts and Sciences* (vol. 26, no. 16 [8 April 1922]: 252).

65 Letter, Clarence H. White to F. Holland Day, 27 October 1912, Norwood.

66 Letter, Walter L. Hervey to the Board of Directors of the Clarence H. White Realty Corporation, 11 September 1922, Gilpin Papers.

67 "School Budget for 1922–23 (June 1, 1922, to June 1, 1923)," Gilpin Papers.

68 Letter, Clarence H. White to Laura Gilpin, 8 November 1922, Gilpin Papers.

69 Letter, Clarence H. White to the Stockholders of the Clarence H. White Realty Corporation, 21 November 1922, Gilpin Papers.

70 Letter, Clarence H. White to Laura Gilpin, 8 November 1922, Gilpin Papers; this philosophy was presented by White's colleague, Paul L. Anderson, in "Where Are We to Get Our Pictorialists?" *Platinum Print*, vol. 1, no. 5 (August 1914): 9.

71 Letter, Clarence H. White to Alfred Stieglitz, 17 April 1901, Stieglitz Archive.

72 "Photographer's Holiday," 139.

73 "A Letter from Clarence White," *Abel's Photographic Weekly*, vol. 32, no. 824 (6 October 1923): 388.

74 [John Heins], "Paper which John Heins used in writing his thesis which was on Clarence White and his work . . . " typescript, undated, White Collection, Princeton.

75 "Article by Arthur Chapman" (note 25 above).

76 John Wallace Gillies, "Amateurs I Have Known, Clarence H. White," *American Photography*, vol. 9, no. 7 (July 1915): 424.

77 John Wallace Gillies, "Amateurs I Have Known," *American Photography*, vol. 9, no. 4 (April 1915): 218.

78 *Dorothea Lange, The Making of a Documentary Photographer*, Interview by

Suzanne Riess, Regional Oral History Office, Bancroft Library, University of California, Berkeley, 1968, 38–39, 44.

79 Anton Bruehl, interview with Peter C. Bunnell, 7 July 1960, quoted in Bunnell, *Reverence*, 11–12.

80 Edward R. Dickson, "Clarence H. White—A Teacher of Photography," *Photo-Era*, vol. 30, no. 1 (January 1913): 3–4.

81 Letter, James N. Giridlian to Clarence H. White, 12 September 1918, White Collection, Princeton.

82 Henry Hoyt Moore, "Photography With A Difference," *The Outlook*, vol. 114 (13 September 1916), 97–98. Jane White recorded in "Photographer's Holiday," 101, that the article was so popular that Moore had it reprinted in a booklet format, which had a wide circulation.

83 Riggins, "Modern Pictorial Photography" (note 13 above), 12–15.

84 Letter carbon copy, unsigned [Walter L. Hervey and Laura Gilpin], "To The Friends of Clarence H. White," undated [January 1926], Gilpin Papers. The authorship of the letter is according to an unsigned letter carbon copy from Laura Gilpin to Mrs. [Doris] Ulman[n], 27 January 1926, Gilpin Papers.

85 "Photographer's Holiday," 138.

86 Riggins, "Modern Pictorial Photography," 19.

87 Letter (typescript translation), Alfred Stieglitz to Heinrich Kühn, 25 August 1925, Stieglitz Archive.

88 Letter, Jane Felix White to Miss [Laura] Gilpin, undated [March 1926], Gilpin Papers.

89 Letter, Jane Felix White to Miss [Laura] Gilpin, undated [May/June 1926], Gilpin Papers.

90 Letter, Jane Felix White to Miss [Laura] Gilpin, 6 February 1927, Gilpin Papers.

91 Letter, Jane Felix White to F. Holland Day, 4 January 1928, Norwood.

92 M. P. White 1975, 246. Clarence H. White Jr. was consistently referred to as Clarence H. White II in White school publications.

93 Clarence H. White [Jr.], resumés, ca. 1943 and 10 February 1949, White Collection, Princeton.

94 Letter, Jane Felix White to F. Holland Day, 26 January 1917, Norwood.

95 M. P. White 1975, 247, with no citation of source, which may have been Jane Felix White's diary, now in the collection of M. P. White.

96 See M. P. White 1975, 256–58.

97 Clarence H. White [Jr.], resumé, 10 February 1949.

98 Sabine, "Mrs. Stella F. Simon" (note 60 above), 235.

BIOGRAPHIES   *Kathleen A. Erwin*

The following biographies of Clarence H. White's colleagues, and of teachers and students at the White School whose work is included in the exhibition rely in many instances on secondary sources. Approximate dates are indicated by ca.; uncertain information by (?). Published references with further information are cited as appropriate.

Short forms of organizations and exhibitions used in the Biographies section (group exhibitions at the Art Center, the Brooklyn Institute, and the White School are not listed).

ART CENTER
Art Center, New York, New York.

BIAS
Brooklyn Institute of Arts and Sciences.

BUFFALO 1910
International Exhibition of Pictorial Photography, Albright Art Gallery, Buffalo, 3 November–1 December 1910.

CAMERA PICTURES
Camera Pictures. New York: Alumni Association, Clarence H. White School of Photography, 1924, 1925.

EHRICH GALLERIES 1914 *
An International Exhibition of Pictorial Photography, Ehrich Art Galleries, New York, 19 January–4 February 1914.

EHRICH GALLERIES 1915 *
An Exhibition of Pictorial Photography, The Print Gallery (under the direction of Ehrich Art Galleries), New York, 1–18 December 1915.

KOHAKAI 1922
First International Kohakai Salon of Photography, Kobe, Osaka, Kyoto, and Tokyo, Japan, May–July 1922. Group of photographs by White School students and alumni selected for exhibition by Margaret Watkins, school instructor.

MONTROSS 1912 *
An Exhibition Illustrating the Progress of the Art of Photography in America, Montross Art Galleries, New York, 10–31 October 1912.

NEWARK 1911*
Modern Photography, Newark Museum Association, Free Public Library, Newark, New Jersey, 6 April–4 May 1911.

PHILADELPHIA 1915 *
An Exhibition Illustrating the Progress of the Art of Photography in America, Rosenbach Galleries, Philadelphia, January 1915.

PPA
Pictorial Photographers of America

RPS 1914
The Royal Photographic Society of Great Britain, Fifty-Ninth Annual Exhibition, London, 24 August–3 October 1914.

RPS 1915
The Royal Photographic Society of Great Britain, Sixtieth Annual Exhibition, London, 23 August–2 October 1915.

WHITE SCHOOL *
Clarence H. White School of Photography, New York.

* *Exhibitions arranged by Clarence White circle.*

PAUL L. ANDERSON
American (born Trenton, New Jersey) 1880–1956

Trained and worked as an electrical engineer until 1910. Began photographing in 1907; opened a portrait studio in East Orange, New Jersey, 1910. Published abundantly on compositional theory and photographic technique, which he taught at White School 1914–18. *Pictorial Photography, Its Principles and Practice* (1917) developed from his lectures at White School. Work appeared in *Vanity Fair* 1914, 1915. PPA member by June 1917. Exhibited: Buffalo 1910 (open section); Newark 1911; Montross 1912; BIAS 1913 (solo); Ehrich Galleries 1914; RPS 1914; BIAS 1916 (solo).

Bender, Donna, comp. *Paul Anderson: Photographs.* Guide Series, no. 7. Tucson: Center for Creative Photography, University of Arizona, 1983.

Pitts, Terence. *Paul Lewis Anderson, A Life in Photography.* The Archive, Research Series, no. 18. Tucson: Center for Creative Photography, University of Arizona, 1983.

MARIE RIGGINS HIGBEE AVERY
American (born Andover, Missouri) 1892–1980

White's student at Teachers College 1919–20, White summer school student 1922. Master's degree from Teachers College 1924. Ph.D. dissertation, Western Reserve University, Cleveland, 1943, "Modern Pictorial Photography and the Measure of Its Art," included a 19-page "word picture of Clarence White's School of Photography at Canaan, Connecticut, in the early 1920's." Taught art and subsequently head of the art department at Hathaway Brown School, Cleveland, 1921–44. Married in 1946 William T. Higbee (d. 1956); married in 1964 Harold T. Avery (d. 1974). Secretary and director of the Foundation for Research on the Nature of Man, Durham, North Carolina.

ALLIE BRAMBERG BODE
American (born Panama, Nebraska) 1891–1975

Secretary of White School ca. 1921–25. White School student ca. 1924–25(?); on photographic study trip to Mexico with Clarence White summer 1925. Work appeared in *Camera Pictures* 1925. PPA corresponding secretary 1926–29. Married G. H. Bode ca. 1927. Exhibited: Art Center 1926 (solo); BIAS 1929 (solo).

FRANCES BODE
American (born Dobbs Ferry, New York) 1892–1974

White's student at Teachers College by 1919; White School student 1921–22. Secretary, White School Alumni Association, 1924; work appeared in *Camera Pictures* 1925. Member PPA 1922–ca. 1952; PPA treasurer 1928–29. Own studio early 1920s, portrait and fashion photography. Traveled around world 1929–30. Social worker 1930s and 1940s. Exhibited: Kohakai 1922.

FRANCESCA S. BOSTWICK
American (born Syracuse, New York) 1872–1967

Named Fannie May Stone at birth; married Charles Byron Bostwick (d. 1914). White's student at Teachers College 1915; White School student 1916–17. Taught pictorial photography at New London (Connecticut) College for Women ca. 1915 until at least 1917. "The Camera as a Messenger from Woods and Fields," with photographs by Bostwick, published in *The Craftsman* October 1916. PPA member by June 1917. Chief interior decorator for Lord & Taylor, New York, 1939–52. Exhibited: Buffalo 1910 (open section); Newark 1911; Montross 1912; BIAS 1913 (two-person exhibition with Amy Whittemore); Ehrich Galleries 1914; RPS 1914.

MARGARET BOURKE-WHITE
American (born New York, New York) 1904–1971

White's student in course offered by Teachers College at White School during 1921–22. Joined PPA 1929. Did industrial photography in Cleveland before coming to New York in 1929 to work for *Fortune* and *Life* magazines from their founding. Collaborated with writer Erskine Caldwell (to whom she was married 1939–42) on *You Have Seen Their Faces* 1937 and *Say, Is This the U.S.A.* 1941.

Goldberg, Vicki. *Margaret Bourke-White: A Biography.* New York: Harper & Row, 1986.

HENRIETTA KIBBE BRIGGS
American

White's student at Teachers College ca. 1912. By 1914 had studio in Portland, Oregon, and exhibition at Portland Art Museum. Married Kenneth Briggs by 1916.

BIOGRAPHIES

ANNE W. BRIGMAN
American (born Honolulu, Hawaii) 1869–1950

Named Anne Wardrope Nott at birth; known as Annie until 1911. Moved to California 1886. Married sea captain Martin Brigman 1894; accompanied him on many voyages; separated from him 1910. Became associate member of Photo-Secession 1903; fellow of the Photo-Secession 1906. Work appeared in *Camera Work* 1909–13; *Vanity Fair* 1914, 1916, 1918. Elected member of Linked Ring, the British photographic secession group, early 1909. Made her only visit to the east coast 1910. White summer school student 1910. *Songs of a Pagan*, book of poems and photographs by Brigman, published 1949. Exhibited: Buffalo 1910.

Ehrens, Susan. *A Poetic Vision: The Photographs of Anne Brigman*. Santa Barbara: Museum of Art, 1995.

BEATRICE A. BROWN
Canadian (born Regina, Saskatchewan) 1897–(?)

White School student 1924–25. Her photograph of fellow students at work at White School reproduced in *Camera Pictures* 1925 and in later school catalogues.

GERTRUDE LEROY BROWN
American (born Chicago, Illinois) 1870(?)–1934

After her parents died ca. 1871, taken in by Charles and Celia F. Brown as if their own daughter, but did not know this until Mrs. Brown, who was dying, told her ca. 1896. No one since, including Gertrude Brown herself, able to verify details of her birth. Earned bachelor's and master's degrees and pursued postgraduate studies in philosophy, political economy, and English literature at Northwestern University, Evanston, Illinois, 1892–95. Cataloguer at Evanston Free Public Library, concentrating on music, a personal interest, 1895–1934. White summer school student ca. 1913; White School student 1915–16. PPA member by June 1917. Work appeared in *Camera Pictures* 1924. Continued to exhibit photographs. Exhibited: Ehrich Galleries 1915.

ANTON BRUEHL
American (born Hawker, Australia) 1900–1982

Came to the United States 1919. PPA member by 1923(?). Left job as engineer at Western Electric Company to study with White privately, then as White School student 1923–24. Work appeared in *Camera Pictures* 1924. White School instructor in studio practice, evening courses, and summer school 1924–26; White School board of advisors ca. 1933–42. In partnership with brother Martin, successful commercial photographer and chief color photographer for Condé Nast's *Vogue* and *Vanity Fair*. Naturalized U.S. citizen 1940. Exhibited: Art Center 1926 (solo); Film und Foto, Stuttgart, Germany, 1929; White School 1940/1941 (solo).

ARTHUR D. CHAPMAN
American, ca. 1882–after 1954

Newspaper printer. White summer school student 1910, 1912(?); White School student 1915–17. Co-director of White New York City summer school 1921. Work appeared in *Camera Pictures* 1924. Published booklet "Greenwich Village; Eight Portraits by Arthur D. Chapman" 1915; article "Travel," *American Annual of Photography*, 1918. Traveled to Canada, Central America, and Grand Canyon. PPA member by June 1917. Moved from Greenwich Village, New York City, to New Jersey, following service in Signal Corps during World War I. Specialized in photographing fungi. Exhibited: Montross 1912; Ehrich Galleries 1914; RPS 1914; RPS 1915; BIAS 1916 (two-person exhibition).

ALFRED A. COHN
American (born Brooklyn, New York) 1897–1972

Known to his friends as Jimmie. White School student 1917–18. Vice president, White School Alumni Association, 1921. Lived in Woodstock, New York, where he taught White summer schools 1931–33. Staff representative for alumni and taught commercial photographic technique and practice at White School ca. 1940–42. Operated commercial photography studio, sometimes with fellow White student August Krug; their work reproduced in such publications as *Vogue* and *Saturday Evening Post*. Moved to Arizona 1943; founded Arizona School of Photography, Tucson, 1948, which perpetuated many of the practices of the White School.

DOROTHY DENNISON
American

White School student 1924. As a member of an American family that had been living many years in Mexico City, helped Clarence White plan a photographic study trip to Mexico summer of 1925.

EDWARD R. DICKSON

Ecuadorian (born Quito) ca. 1880–1922

First came to United States 1903. Worked for Marine Engine Corporation, later merged with Otis Elevator Company, New York; quit to devote himself to creative photography in 1917. White summer school student 1910; White's student at Teachers College 1912–13; White School student 1917. Work appeared posthumously in *Camera Pictures* 1924. Taught at White School at unknown date. Published *Platinum Print* 1913–17; work appeared in and edited *Poems of the Dance* 1921; articles on photographic composition in *American Annual of Photography* 1920, 1921. PPA member by June 1917; secretary PPA 1917–20. Exhibited: Newark 1911 (arranged exhibition); Montross 1912; BIAS 1913 (solo); Ehrich Galleries 1914; BIAS 1914 (solo); RPS 1914; RPS 1915; Philadelphia 1915.

JOHN A. FUNK JR.

American (born Akron, Ohio) 1895/97–1964

Studied art in Akron, Chicago, Atlanta, and New York. Did art work in advertising departments of Goodyear and Firestone in Akron; did advertising photography for Underwood & Underwood, New York. White School evening student 1932–33. Work appeared in *U.S. Camera* 1935, 1937. Art editor of *Scribner's Magazine* 1937–38, *Country Gentleman* 1940–55, and *Furrow* 1955–62. Exhibited: National Alliance of Art and Industry, New York, 1932, 1934.

LAURA GILPIN

American (born Austin Bluffs, Colorado) 1891–1979

White School student 1916–17. Secretary, White School Alumni Association, 1917. Work appeared in *Camera Pictures* 1924. PPA member by June 1917; PPA regional vice president 1928 until at least 1932. Commercial photographer, Colorado Springs 1918–42. Public relations photographer for Boeing, Wichita, Kansas, 1942–44. Lived in Santa Fe, New Mexico, 1945–79. Published photographically illustrated books: *The Pueblos* 1941; *Temples in Yucatan* 1948; *The Rio Grande* 1949; *The Enduring Navaho* 1968. Exhibited: White School 1921 (solo); Art Center 1924 (solo).

Sandweiss, Martha A. *Laura Gilpin: An Enduring Grace*. Fort Worth: Amon Carter Museum, 1986.

JAMES N. GIRIDLIAN

American (born Kayseri, Turkey) 1893–1969

Schoolmate of Clarence White's son Maynard at Stuyvesant School, New York, where Giridlian won school camera club prize to attend White summer school 1913; White School student 1914–16. Photography studio in Elmhurst, New York, 1915. U.S. Navy 1917–19; officer in charge of photographic instruction in the Navy and Marine Corps. PPA member by June 1917. Lived in California from at least 1920; movie second cameraman ca. 1927 until at least 1930; architectural photographer. Prominent horticulturist in Pasadena and Arcadia, California. Exhibited: Ehrich Galleries 1914; Philadelphia 1915.

LOUISE HALSEY

American (born Jersey City, New Jersey) 1872–1962

Named Louise Edwards at birth. By 1900 married James Harvey Halsey (d. 1902) and moved to Metuchen, New Jersey. Took up photography in 1907. White's student at Columbia 1907–12; White School student 1916–17. Portrait studio in New Brunswick, New Jersey, at least until 1914/15. Exhibited: Newark 1911; Montross 1912.

Palmquist, Peter E. *Louise E. Halsey: An American Pictorialist*. Arcata, California: Reese Bullen Gallery, Humboldt State University, 1985.

PAUL B. HAVILAND

French (born Paris) 1880–1950

New York representative of father's china manufacturing firm, Haviland & Co. 1901–15. Began photographing seriously ca. 1908. Strong, loyal supporter of Alfred Stieglitz from 1908; named associate member of Photo-Secession 1908, fellow 1909; work appeared in *Camera Work* 1909–14; wrote for *Camera Work* 1909–15; associate editor of *Camera Work* 1910–17. Private student of Clarence White 1909, broke off with White 1912 because of estrangement between Stieglitz and White. Returned to France 1915 and continued in father's business. Portrait photographer 1929–30; later a winegrower. Exhibited: Buffalo 1910 (open section).

JOHN P. HEINS

American (born New York, New York) 1896–1969

White's student at Teachers College ca. 1919, where earned B.S. 1919 and M.A. 1939. Taught composition, metalwork, and jewelry at Teachers College 1919–30, and art appreciation and design at White School 1920–42. Freelance commercial designer, printmaker, painter. With Lewis F. White and others, ran Equinox Cooperative Press in mid-1930s. Professor of art, Skidmore College, Saratoga Springs, New York 1943–64.

ANTOINETTE B. HERVEY
American (born Gilbertsville, New York) 1857–1945

Named Antoinette Bryant at birth. Married Walter L. Hervey 1887, after which lived in Brooklyn, then Manhattan. Photographed comprehensive record of the Cathedral of St. John the Divine, New York, and its construction ca. 1900–38; *The Word in Stone* ca. 1924, with photogravures of Hervey's images, published to promote fund raising for the cathedral. White School student 1915–16; White's student at Teachers College 1917–20. President, White School Alumni Association, 1921; vice president 1925. Work appeared in *Camera Pictures* 1925. PPA member by June 1917; chairman PPA monthly print competition ca. 1919–24; PPA vice president 1925; honorary vice president from ca. 1938. Art Center board 1924–26. Exhibited: White School 1921 (solo); Art Center 1925 (solo).

GEORGE BUELL HOLLISTER
American (born Brooklyn, New York) 1865–1952

Worked for Corning Glass Works from 1904, becoming a vice president and director of the company. Photographed with his second wife, Hebe (they signed their work jointly), whom he married in 1911. PPA member by June 1917. Possibly attended White summer school 1917; on 1925 list of White School alumni. Spent much of retirement in Bermuda. Exhibited 1917–22, including Pittsburgh Salon.

MILLIE E. HOOPS
American, died after 1935

Probably Mrs. Frank A. Hoops. White summer school student 1918(?); White School student 1918–19; White's student at Teachers College by 1919. PPA member by July 1920. Moved from Boston to California ca. 1922.

BERNARD S. HORNE
American (born Pittsburgh, Pennsylvania) 1867–1933

Graduate of Princeton University 1890. Lived in Princeton, New Jersey, from ca. 1912. White School student 1915–16. President, White School Alumni Association, 1917, 1924; work appeared in *Camera Pictures* 1924, 1925 (only alumnus with work reproduced in both volumes; publication due to his interest and enthusiasm). Taught photographic technique at White School 1918–28. PPA member by June 1917. Exhibited: White School 1920 (solo); Art Center 1926 (solo; works grouped in series from pure design to the application of design to still life, portraiture, and landscape).

Goldberg, Vicki. *A Catalogue of Design Photographs by Bernard Shea Horne.* New York: Keith Douglas de Lellis, 1986.

HANS L. JORGENSEN
American (born Omaha, Nebraska) 1915–

White School student 1937–38. Treasurer, White School Alumni Association, 1941. Worked for fashion photographer Louise Dahl-Wolfe. Hired by *Harper's Bazaar* as photographic assistant to George Hoyningen-Huene. Work published in *Harper's Bazaar*, *Jr. Bazaar*, and *Good Housekeeping*. Motion picture cameraman in U.S. Army Signal Corps during World War II. Did fashion and other commercial photography in own studio in Seattle, Washington; clients included Seattle department store Frederick & Nelson.

DOROTHEA LANGE
American (born Hoboken, New Jersey) 1895–1965

Named Dorothea Nutzhorn at birth; from 1918 used her mother's maiden name, Lange. Trained to be a teacher at Teachers College ca. 1913–14. White's student at Teachers College 1914–15, per list of White's TC students in White Collection, Princeton; 1917–18, per Lange's application for a Guggenheim fellowship. Did not complete any of White's assignments. Worked in various photographers' studios, including that of Arnold Genthe, New York, 1914–15. Opened portrait studio in San Francisco 1919. Began photographing the effects of the Depression in the 1930s. Worked for the Farm Security Administration 1935–39. With husband Paul S. Taylor, published *An American Exodus* 1939. Photographed for *Life* 1954–63.

Meltzer, Milton. *Dorothea Lange: A Photographer's Life.* New York: Farrar Straus Giroux, 1978.

KENNETH A. LINN

American (born New York, New York) 1906–1981

White School student 1930–31; White School staff 1931–42; associate director in charge of studio work 1940–42. Taught photography in the Signal Corps Photographic School, Fort Monmouth, New Jersey, 1942.

FLORENCE BURTON LIVINGSTON

American

Mrs. Florence Burton Livingston was White's student at Teachers College 1913–14; White School student 1916–17. Living in California 1925. Exhibited: Ehrich Galleries 1915.

DANIEL E. LUND

American

Possibly White School student ca. 1919; included on list of White School alumni compiled in 1925, when he was living in New York City.

JULIA MARSHALL

American (born Duluth, Minnesota) 1897–1994

White School student 1921–22, 1927. Work appeared in *Camera Pictures* 1924. Distinguished Duluth, Minnesota, philanthropist. Exhibited: Kohakai 1922.

IRA W. MARTIN

American (born Lennon, Michigan) 1886–1960

Studied art Santa Barbara, California, ca. 1910. Photographer, Signal Corps, 1918. Subsequently lived in New York City environs. White School student 1918–19. Work appeared in *Camera Pictures* 1924. Aerial photographer 1919. Worked two years for advertising art firm Stanford Briggs ca. 1920–22. Work appeared in *Vanity Fair* 1921 (abstract photographs), 1929. Joined PPA 1921; chairman PPA monthly print competition 1924–26; held various PPA offices, including president 1927–37; director of international salons 1927 until at least 1942. Photographer for Frick Art Reference Library, New York, 1923–60. Taught advanced pictorialism at Brooklyn Institute 1935–37 and photographic composition for PPA 1937–40. Exhibited: White School 1922 (solo); Art Center 1924 (solo); Art Center 1927 (solo).

PAUL OUTERBRIDGE JR.

American (born New York, New York) 1896–1958

Student at Art Students League 1915. Student and temporary lecturer at White School 1921–22; adjunct member of White School staff ca. 1933. Joined PPA 1922. Work appeared in *Vanity Fair* 1922; *Camera Pictures* 1924. Successful commercial photographer in United States before photographing in Europe 1925–29. Lived in New York 1929–43; in 1930s, highly successful commercial color photographer. Lived in California; continued to photograph 1943–58. Exhibited: Art Center 1924 (solo); Film und Foto, Stuttgart, Germany, 1929.

Barryte, Bernard, Graham Howe, and Elaine Dines. *Paul Outerbridge: A Singular Aesthetic*. Laguna Beach: Museum of Art, 1981.

JANE REECE

American (born near West Jefferson, Ohio) 1868–1961

Portrait photographer in Dayton, Ohio, from 1904. White's student at Columbia 1909. PPA member by June 1917. Large collection of her work in Dayton Art Institute.

Pinkney, Helen L. "Jane Reece Memorial Exhibition: 'The Wonderful World of Photography.'" *The Dayton Art Institute Bulletin*, vol. 21, no. 5 (March–April 1963).

WYNN RICHARDS

American (born Greenville, Mississippi) 1888–1960

Named Martha Wynn at birth; used maiden and married surnames professionally. White School student 1918–19, 1923. Member PPA. Photographed for *Vogue* 1923. Based in Chicago 1924–28 doing advertising photography in partnership with fellow White School alumna Bettie Frear. Successful commercial photographer and a leading figure in the fashion community, New York, 1928–48. In 1932, married second husband G. H. Taylor, who served as her manager and edited *My Best Photograph and Why* 1937, profiling photographers including Richards and other White alumni. Photographed for Cotton Council 1943–50s. Resettled in Greenville 1948.

Yochelson, Bonnie. *Wynn Richards*. New York: Photofind Gallery, 1989.

BIOGRAPHIES

HENRY W. SHEPARD
American (born Buffalo, New York) ca. 1893–1953

White's student 1924–25. Organized photography department of Seneca Vocational High School, Buffalo, 1927, and served as its head until his death.

STELLA F. SIMON
American (born Charleston, South Carolina) 1878–1973

Interest in photography intensified after the death of her husband in 1917. White School student 1923(?)–25. President, White School Alumni Association, 1925; work appeared in *Camera Pictures* 1925; on photographic study trip to Mexico with Clarence White summer 1925. In Germany ca. 1928 made experimental film *Hands*, emphasizing pattern and showing only hands. Opened commercial and advertising studio in Manhattan 1931. Secretary PPA 1929 until at least 1932. Exhibited: Art Center 1931 (solo).

CLARA E. SIPPRELL
American (born Tilsonburg, Ontario, Canada) 1885–1975

Moved to Buffalo, New York, by 1896. Brother's partner in photo studio in Buffalo 1905–15. White summer school student 1913. In 1914 opened studio in Lake Placid, New York, with Ellen J. Windsor; Sipprell and Windsor attended White School 1916–17. From 1915 lived in New York City in winter and Vermont in summer. PPA member by June 1917; member Royal Photographic Society. Traveled extensively in Europe. Naturalized U.S. citizen 1944. Exhibited: BIAS 1914 (three-person exhibition, with Edith R. Wilson and Imogen Cunningham).

McCabe, Mary Kennedy. *Clara Sipprell: Pictorial Photographer*. Fort Worth: Amon Carter Museum, 1990.

FRANCES SPALDING
American (born Denver, Colorado) 1896–1979

White School student ca. 1921–22. Joined PPA 1922. Vice president, White School Alumni Association, 1924; work appeared in *Camera Pictures* 1925. Photographer and Curator of Records for Hispanic Society of America, New York, 1922–79. Exhibited: Kohakai 1922.

EMA SPENCER
American (born Brownsville, Ohio) 1857–1941

Founding member of Newark (Ohio) Camera Club 1898. Shared studio in Newark, Ohio, with White. Listed as associate member of Photo-Secession 1909. Work reproduced in *Camera Work* 1909. Portrait photographer in Newark. Columnist for *Newark Advocate*. Exhibited: Buffalo 1910; Newark 1911; Montross 1912; BIAS 1914 (solo); RPS 1914.

RALPH STEINER
American (born Cleveland, Ohio) 1899–1986

Studied photography at Dartmouth College. White School student 1921–22; White helped get job making photogravure plates at Manhattan Photogravure Company 1922. White School advisor ca. 1933–36. Work appeared in *Vanity Fair* 1928. Career encompassed film making, editing, and commercial photography, as well as art photography. Exhibited: Film und Foto, Stuttgart, Germany, 1929.

Steiner, Ralph. *A Point of View*. Middletown: Wesleyan University Press, 1978.

KARL STRUSS
American (born New York, New York) 1886–1981

White's student at Columbia evenings 1908–12; special student at White School 1915–16. White School advisor 1914–16. Became final member of Photo-Secession 1912. Work appeared in *Camera Work* 1912; *Vanity Fair* 1915–17. Taught photography at Columbia University summer 1912. Taught photography at Brooklyn Institute 1916. Worked in father's factory until 1914; own studio from 1914, doing portrait, magazine, and advertising photography. Marketed Struss Pictorial Lens from 1914. PPA member by June 1917. After military service during World War I, went to Hollywood, where he pioneered artistic cinematography, winning first Academy Award for *Sunrise* 1926. Exhibited: Buffalo 1910 (open section); Newark 1911; Teachers College 1912 (*Photographs of New York City*); Montross 1912; BIAS 1912–13 (solo); Ehrich Galleries 1914; RPS 1914; Philadelphia 1915; RPS 1915; Ehrich Galleries 1915.

McCandless, Barbara, Bonnie Yochelson, and Richard Koszarski. *New York to Hollywood: The Photography of Karl Struss*. Fort Worth: Amon Carter Museum, 1995.

EDITH WINIFRED TAIT
American (born Norfolk, Virginia) 1901–1991

White School student 1925–26. Lived in Montreat, North Carolina, from 1932, painting and writing, as well as photographing. Her travel book *The Other Penny* 1968 illustrated with her photographs.

EVERETT S. TURNER
American (born Meriden, Connecticut) ca. 1900–1934

White School student 1920–21. Photographer in New Britain, Connecticut,1924–34. Exhibited: Kohakai 1922.

DORIS ULMANN (JAEGER)
American (born New York, New York) ca. 1882–1934

White's student at Teachers College 1915(?)–19(?). White School student 1915–18. Work appeared in *Camera Pictures* 1924. By 1915 married Dr. Charles Jaeger, later also a White student and active in PPA; by 1921 Ulmann resumed use of maiden name; divorced 1925. PPA member by June 1917. Published three books of photogravure portraits of prominent people 1920, 1922, 1925; subsequently concentrated on photographing people in rural areas. Photographs illustrated *Roll, Jordan, Roll* 1934. Ulmann, independently wealthy, never accepted fees for her work. Exhibited: White School 1920 (solo); Art Center 1926 (solo).

Featherstone, David. *Doris Ulmann, American Portraits.* Albuquerque: University of New Mexico Press, 1985.

HOWARD R. VAN RYN
American (born Wilkinsburg, Pennsylvania) 1891–1968

Born, lived, and died in Wilkinsburg, Pennsylvania. On class list of White School for 1918–19, at which time serving in U.S. army; Federal Board for Vocational Education student at White School 1922. Exhibited: Kohakai 1922.

MARY LACY VAN WAGENEN
American (born New York State) ca. 1886–(?)

White's student at Teachers College 1915–16; White School student 1916–17. PPA member by June 1917. Living in Orange, New Jersey, ca. 1917; New York City in 1925.

ROBERT WAIDA
Japanese, 1889–after 1960

Adopted name Robert Waida as anglicization of I. Ueda. White School student 1921–22. White School staff 1926–32, teaching studio practice. Joined PPA 1923. Work appeared in *Camera Pictures* 1924. Manhattan studio, successfully specialized in advertising still lifes and portraits; work appeared in *Vogue*. Returned to Japan in 1932. Established portrait studio in Manila 1933. Lived in Kobe, Japan, from 1934 until at least 1960. Exhibited: Kohakai 1922; White School 1926 (solo); Art Center 1927 (solo).

JOSEPHINE M. WALLACE
American (born Davenport, Iowa) ca. 1868–1960

Member of prominent agricultural family. Aspired to be opera singer; became interested in photography after her singing voice failed. White School student 1917–18; White summer school student 1920, 1924(?). For many years operated a portrait studio in Des Moines. Moved to Tucson in 1935; member of Tucson Camera Club and Tucson Fine Arts Association. Exhibited in Japan, Australia, Canada, and France, as well as United States.

MARGARET WATKINS
Canadian (born Hamilton, Ontario) 1884–1969

Named Meta Gladys Watkins at birth; known as Margaret after left home. White summer school student 1914; White School student ca. 1917. White School staff ca. 1919–ca. 1923; White summer school staff 1925. Work appeared in *Camera Pictures* 1924. Assistant to photographer Alice Boughton for a year sometime during ca. 1915–19. Work appeared in *Vanity Fair* 1921. PPA member by 1918; PPA corresponding secretary 1918, 1920; vice president 1926–27. Art Center board 1926–27. Essay "Advertising and Photography," *Pictorial Photography in America*, 1926. Studio in Greenwich Village, portraits and still life studies for advertising. Abandoned photographic career and left United States to live in Scotland with aunts 1928. Exhibited: Kohakai 1922; Art Center 1923 (solo).

Beloff, Halla, Joseph Mulholland, and Lori Pauli. *Margaret Watkins, 1884–1969: Photographs.* Glasgow: Street Level Photography Gallery, 1994.

Mulholland, Joseph. "A Sad Strange Gleam of Vision," *The Photographic Collector*, vol. 3, no. 1 (spring 1982): 50-63.

CLARENCE H. WHITE

American (born West Carlisle, Ohio) 1871–1925

Bookkeeper in Newark, Ohio, until 1904. Elected member of Linked Ring, the British photographic secession group, 1900. Founding member of Photo-Secession 1902. Work appeared in *Camera Work* 1903–10; *Vanity Fair* 1915; elsewhere. Moved to New York City 1906. Taught art photography for Columbia University 1907–25 and for Brooklyn Institute of Arts and Sciences 1908–22. Taught art photography in summers 1910–25: Georgetown Island, Maine 1910–15; East Canaan, Connecticut 1916; Canaan, Connecticut 1917–24; Mexico 1925. Head of the Clarence H. White School of Photography, New York, 1914–25. Founding member PPA; PPA president 1917–21. On committee to create Art Center; member of Art Center board 1920–23. Exhibited: BIAS 1909 (solo); Buffalo 1910; Newark 1911; Montross 1912; BIAS 1913 (solo); Ehrich Galleries 1914; RPS 1914; BIAS 1914 (solo); RPS 1915; Ehrich Galleries 1915; Art Center 1926 (memorial); White School 1942 (memorial).

Bunnell, Peter C. *Clarence H. White: The Reverence for Beauty.* Athens: Ohio University Gallery of Fine Art, 1986.

White, Maynard P. *Clarence H. White.* Millerton, New York: Aperture, 1979.

Homer, William Innes, ed. *Symbolism of Light: The Photographs of Clarence H. White.* Wilmington: Delaware Art Museum, 1977.

AMY WHITTEMORE

American (born Cleveland, Ohio) 1875–1959

White's student at Teachers College 1912–13; White's student at Brooklyn Institute 1914; White School student 1916–17. Work appeared in *Harper's Bazar* November 1915. PPA member by June 1917. Art teacher. Whittemore's addresses included New Jersey, Maine, Massachusetts, New York, Connecticut, South Carolina, North Carolina; she also visited California, Switzerland, and Austria. Exhibited: Buffalo 1910 (open section); Newark 1911; Montross 1912; BIAS 1913 (two-person exhibition with Francesca Bostwick); RPS 1914; Ehrich Galleries 1914; Ehrich Galleries 1915.

EDITH R. WILSON

American, 1864–1924

White summer school student 1910(?), 1914, 1922; White School student 1916–17. Work appeared in *Camera Pictures* 1925. PPA member by June 1917. Illustrated *Everychild's Mother Goose* 1918. Educator. Lived in Mount Vernon, New York. Exhibited: Newark 1911; Montross 1912; Ehrich Galleries 1914; BIAS 1914 (three-person exhibition with Clara Sipprell and Imogen Cunningham).

ESTELLE WOLF

American (born Evart, Michigan) 1886–1988

Attended Simmons College, Boston. Moved to New York City during the Depression. White School student 1931–32. Formed photographic partnership Grinnell-Wolf, possibly with White School classmate Peter Grinnell. Community activist in New York City.

MILDRED R. WOODS

American (born Glenwood, Iowa) 1902–1983

On 1925 list of White School alumni. From 1937, lived in New Mexico, where she was a professional photographer. Partner in the Warner-Woods Portrait Studio in Albuquerque 1940–68.

PAUL J. WOOLF

(born London, England) 1899–1985

A.B. from University of California at Berkeley ca. 1928. White School student 1931–32. Successful commercial photographer, with own Manhattan studio for portrait, advertising, commercial, industrial, child, night architectural, and pictorial photography, and photo murals. Articles on composition in photography, architectural photography, and night photography. Made photographs to assist work of wife, Margaret E. Fries, M.D., in psychological research. Earned M.S. degree in psychiatric social work ca. 1942; practiced as a psychotherapist.

NOTE ON WHITE SCHOOL CATALOGUES AND PUBLICATIONS

The White School published a wide variety of catalogues, many undated. Dated catalogues include: full-year catalogues for 1914–17, 1919, 1921, 1924, 1940, and 1941; summer school catalogues for 1910, 1914–25, 1934, and 1941 (typescript). The 1921 full-year catalogue was not published separately, but was included in *The Bulletin of the Alumni, Clarence H. White School of Photography*, November 1921. Other dates assigned to catalogues in this book are based on annotations or internal evidence, and in some cases differ from dates assigned by others.

Catalogues can be found in the White Collection, Princeton, with the following exceptions:

1917 full-year catalogue: (Joseph) Mulholland Archive of materials collected by Margaret Watkins, Glasgow, Scotland (Mulholland Archive)

1917 full-year catalogue for only Max Weber's lectures: Joy Weber Collection (reproduced in its entirety in Percy North, *Max Weber, The Cubist Decade, 1910–1920* [Atlanta: High Museum of Art, 1991]: 93)

1918 summer catalogue: Center for Creative Photography, University of Arizona, Tucson

1920 summer catalogue: Study Collection, Department of Photography, The Museum of Modern Art, New York

Undated, ca. 1927–28 full-year catalogue: New York Public Library and Gilpin Papers

Undated, ca. 1938 full-year catalogue: Helen Simmons Faye Collection

Unless otherwise noted, White School catalogues, announcements, schedules, checklists, and alumni publications may be found in the White Collection, Princeton, and are the source for information on school faculty, courses, and other school-related activities. The White Collection, Princeton, also holds lists (which are incomplete) of White's students at Teachers College, and of students and alumni of the White School. Information on attendance, and generalizations about White students found throughout this book are based on these lists.

FREQUENTLY CITED SOURCES

Bunnell, *Reverence*: Peter C. Bunnell. *Clarence H. White: The Reverence for Beauty*. Athens: Ohio University Gallery of Fine Art, 1986.

Gilpin Papers: Laura Gilpin Papers, Amon Carter Museum, Fort Worth, Texas.

M. P. White 1975: Maynard Pressley White Jr. *Clarence H. White: A Personal Portrait*. Ann Arbor: University Microfilms International, 1975.

Memorial: *Clarence H. White School of Photography, A Memorial to Its Founder*, ca. 1939, White Collection, Princeton.

Norwood: F. Holland Day Collection, Norwood Historical Society, Norwood, Massachusetts; also Archives of American Art, Smithsonian Institution, F. Holland Day Papers, lent for filming by the Norwood Historical Society.

"Photographer's Holiday": Jane Felix White, "A Photographer's Holiday," typescript carbon, 1938–39, White Collection, Princeton.

Stieglitz Archive: Stieglitz Archive, Yale Collection of American Literature, Beinecke Rare Book and Manuscript Library, Yale University.

Symbolism of Light: M. P. White. *Symbolism of Light: The Photographs of Clarence H. White* (Newark: Delaware Art Museum, 1977).

White Collection, Princeton: The Clarence H. White Collection at The Art Museum, Princeton University; assembled and organized by Professor Clarence H. White Jr. and given in memory of Lewis F. White, Dr. Maynard P. White Sr., and Professor Clarence H. White Jr., the sons of Clarence H. White Sr. and Jane Felix White. Additional materials received by gift and bequest of Clarence H. White Jr. and Ruth Royer White. Permission to quote given by The Art Museum, Princeton University.

EXHIBITION CHECKLIST

All images in the exhibition are reproduced in this book, and are listed here alphabetically by photographer. Each entry is followed by the page number on which the image appears.

PAUL L. ANDERSON
Pennsylvania Station, New York, 1916
Gelatin silver print on tissue
13 1/16 x 9 15/16 in. (33.1 x 25.2 cm)
Page 86

PAUL L. ANDERSON
Mrs. George B. (Hebe) Hollister, 1917
Gelatin silver print
13 x 10 in. (33.0 x 25.5 cm)
Page 29

MARIE RIGGINS HIGBEE AVERY
Fishermen, 1932
Gelatin silver print
10 1/16 x 9 1/2 in. (25.5 x 24.1 cm)
Page 45

ALLIE BRAMBERG BODE
Cuernavaca, Mexico (Top Hotel Morelos), 1925
Platinum print
9 5/16 x 7 1/16 in. (23.6 x 17.9 cm)
Page 77

ALLIE BRAMBERG BODE
Mexican Boy, 1925
Platinum print
9 1/8 x 7 in. (23.1 x 17.8 cm)
Page 104

ALLIE BRAMBERG BODE
San Francisco Xavier, Seminario de San Martín, Tepotzotlán, Mexico, 1925
Platinum print
9 x 7 1/16 in. (22.8 x 18.0 cm)
Page 79

FRANCES BODE
Printing Room, Clarence H. White School of Photography, 460 W. 144th Street, New York, 1922
Platinum print
4 1/16 x 3 1/8 in. (10.3 x 7.9 cm)
Page 147

FRANCESCA S. BOSTWICK
Bruges, Belgium, ca. 1910
Platinum print
8 1/4 x 6 1/4 in. (20.9 x 15.8 cm)
Page 89

MARGARET BOURKE-WHITE
Coiled Aluminum Rods, 1930
Gelatin silver print
13 1/2 x 10 1/16 in. (34.2 x 25.5 cm)
Page 175

MARGARET BOURKE-WHITE
Organ Pipes, ca. 1931
Gelatin silver print
13 1/2 x 9 1/2 in. (34.2 x 24.2 cm)
Page 165

HENRIETTA KIBBE BRIGGS
Grandmother, ca. 1912
Platinum print
6 9/16 x 4 5/8 in. (16.6 x 11.7 cm)
Page 37

ANNE W. BRIGMAN
Invictus, 1925
Gelatin silver print
9 13/16 x 7 9/16 in. (25.0 x 19.2 cm)
Page 53

BEATRICE A. BROWN
Students at Work in the Exhibition and Lecture Room, Clarence H. White School of Photography, 460 W. 144th Street, New York, 1924/1925
Platinum print
4 5/8 x 3 5/8 in. (11.7 x 9.2 cm)
Page 153

GERTRUDE LEROY BROWN
Clarence H. White, Gertrude Käsebier, and Students of the Seguinland School of Photography, Georgetown Island, Maine, ca. 1913
Platinum print
5 15/16 x 7 7/16 in. (15.1 x 18.9 cm)
Page 120

ANTON BRUEHL
Window and Old Bench, 1924
Platinum print
8 1/16 x 6 1/16 in. (20.4 x 15.4 cm)
Page 139

ANTON BRUEHL
Still Life, Christmas Ornaments, 1925
Gelatin silver print
4 5/8 x 3 13/16 in. (11.7 x 9.6 cm)
Page 169

ANTON BRUEHL
Top Hats (Weber and Heilbroner advertisement), ca. 1929
Gelatin silver print
13 11/16 x 10 3/4 in. (34.8 x 27.3 cm)
Page 164

ANTON AND MARTIN BRUEHL
Resting Model, ca. 1935
Carbro print
14 1/4 x 11 1/4 in. (36.2 x 28.5 cm)
Page 31

ARTHUR D. CHAPMAN
Diagonals (Christopher Street from the 8th Street station of the Sixth Avenue el, New York), 1913
Platinum print
8 1/16 x 6 1/16 in. (20.4 x 15.3 cm)
Page 69

ARTHUR D. CHAPMAN
Max Weber, 1914
Platinum print
8 x 6 1/16 in. (20.4 x 15.4 cm)
Page 101

ALFRED COHN
Puritan Avenue, ca. 1920
Platinum print
8 1/8 x 6 1/8 in. (20.6 x 15.5 cm)
Page 87

DOROTHY DENNISON
Sprouting Bulbs in Bowl (normal; soft; contrasty; brown tone), ca. 1924
Platinum prints
Approximately 3 5/8 x 4 1/2 in. (9.1 x 11.5 cm) each
Page 65

EDWARD R. DICKSON
Design in Nature, ca. 1913
Platinum print
9 x 7 1/2 in. (22.8 x 19.1 cm)
Page 49

JOHN A. FUNK JR.
Rehearsal, ca. 1932
Gelatin silver print
6 1/2 x 6 in. (16.4 x 15.3 cm)
Page 115

Laura Gilpin
White Iris, 1926
Platinum print
9 1/2 x 7 1/8 in. (24.1 x 18.1 cm)
Page 63

Laura Gilpin
Bryce Canyon, Utah, Fall 1930
Gelatin silver print
13 1/4 x 10 3/4 in. (33.6 x 27.3 cm)
Page 51

James N. Giridlian
Still Life, Cup, and Apple, 1914
Cyanotype and red and yellow gum bichromate print on tissue on gilt mount
4 15/16 x 6 15/16 in. (12.5 x 17.6 cm)
Page 67

Louise Halsey
North Gate, Columbia University, and Main and Household Arts Buildings, Teachers College, New York, ca. 1911
Platinum print
7 3/4 x 5 1/16 in. (19.6 x 12.8 cm)
Page 80

Louise Halsey
Volkmar Potter, 1911
Platinum print
7 x 5 in. (17.7 x 12.6 cm)
Page 107

Louise Halsey
Frances Smith in Oriental Costume, 1913
Platinum print
6 1/16 x 7 3/4 in. (15.4 x 19.7 cm)
Page 27

Paul B. Haviland
Young Woman, ca. 1910
Platinum print
9 11/16 x 7 11/16 in. (24.6 x 19.5 cm)
Page 30

John P. Heins
Egg Cup Abstraction, ca. 1919
Platinum print
4 11/16 x 3 13/16 in. (11.8 x 9.6 cm)
Page 171

John P. Heins
Arches and Shadows, ca. 1925
Gelatin silver print
2 5/16 x 1 9/16 in. (5.8 x 4.0 cm)
Page 74

Antoinette B. Hervey
In the Arbor, by 1919
Platinum print
7 1/8 x 9 in. (18.1 x 22.8 cm)
Page 33

Antoinette B. Hervey
Arches of the Municipal Building, New York, by 1920
Palladium print
11 1/4 x 7 3/4 in. (28.5 x 19.7 cm)
Page 75

Antoinette B. Hervey
Base of a Great Column (in the nave of the Cathedral of St. John the Divine, New York), 1929
Platinum print
7 5/8 x 6 9/16 in. (19.4 x 16.6 cm)
Page 71

George Buell Hollister and Hebe Hollister
A Little Girl, ca. 1918
Gelatin silver print
8 5/16 x 6 5/8 in. (21.2 x 16.9 cm)
Page 35

George Buell Hollister and Hebe Hollister
Playmates, ca. 1918
Carbon print
13 1/4 x 10 1/2 in. (33.7 x 26.8 cm)
Page 129

Millie E. Hoops
Practice Hour (One-and-two-and . . .), 1922
Gelatin silver print
8 3/4 x 6 5/8 in. (22.2 x 16.8 cm)
Page 151

Bernard S. Horne
Design—Daffodil, ca. 1917
Platinum print
8 3/16 x 6 1/8 in. (20.8 x 15.5 cm)
Page 61

Bernard S. Horne
Design—Princeton, ca. 1917
Gelatin silver print
11 7/8 x 9 15/16 in. (30.1 x 25.2 cm)
Page 73

Bernard S. Horne
Summer Session, Clarence H. White School of Photography, ca. 1917
Platinum print
8 1/8 x 6 1/8 in. (20.6 x 15.6 cm)
Page 125

Hans L. Jorgensen
Poster for the Exhibition of Photographs by the Students of the Clarence H. White School of Photography Classes of 1937–38 Shown at Rockefeller Center, 1938
Letterpress and collotype
17 1/2 x 11 1/2 in. (44.5 x 29.2 cm)
Page 187

Dorothea Lange
Ex-Slave with a Long Memory, Alabama, 1937
Gelatin silver print
7 5/16 x 9 5/16 in. (18.5 x 23.6 cm)
Page 137

Kenneth A. Linn
Flower Abstract (photogram), 1929
Gelatin silver print
8 5/8 x 6 3/8 in. (22.0 x 16.3 cm)
Page 179

Kenneth A. Linn
Potted Jade Plant, 1930s
Gelatin silver print
3 9/16 x 4 5/8 in. (8.9 x 11.7 cm)
Page 64

Florence B. Livingston
Maid Reading a Letter, ca. 1913–17
Platinum print
9 1/8 x 6 1/2 in. (23.1 x 16.5 cm)
Page 36

Daniel E. Lund
The Pigeons, 1919
Platinum print
4 3/8 x 3 9/16 in. (11.1 x 9.0 cm)
Page 135

Julia Marshall
Hershey's (advertisement), 1922/1927
Satista-gum bichromate print
3 9/16 x 5 1/2 in. (9.1 x 13.9 cm)
Page 183

Ira W. Martin
At the Plaza, New York, ca. 1930
Gelatin silver print
6 9/16 x 4 1/2 in. (16.7 x 11.4 cm)
Page 81

Ira W. Martin
Steel Mill, ca. 1930
Gelatin silver print
9 x 6 7/8 in. (22.8 x 17.4 cm)
Page 111

Ira W. Martin
Clapboard House with Shadows, by 1934
Platinum print
6 9/16 x 4 3/4 in. (16.7 x 12.0 cm)
Page 83

Paul Outerbridge Jr.
Kitchen Table, 1921
Gelatin silver print
9 5/8 x 7 5/8 in. (24.4 x 19.3 cm)
Page 93

Paul Outerbridge Jr.
New York from a Back Window, ca. 1922
Platinum print
4 9/16 x 3 9/16 in. (11.6 x 9.0 cm)
Page 85

EXHIBITION CHECKLIST

PAUL OUTERBRIDGE JR.
Still Life, Cheese, and Crackers, 1922
Platinum print
4½ x 3⅝ in. (11.4 x 9.2 cm)
Page 97

PAUL OUTERBRIDGE JR.
Nude Female Sitting at Dressing Table,
ca. 1936
Carbro print
15¾ x 11⅞ in. (40.0 x 30.2 cm)
Page 25

JANE REECE
Spaces (Harry Losée), 1922
Gelatin silver print on tissue
9⅝ x 7⅝ in. (24.4 x 19.3 cm)
Page 22

WYNN RICHARDS
*Still Life—Candlestick, Flowers in a Vase,
Books, and Scissors*, ca. 1918
Cyanotype on tissue
6¾ x 4¾ in. (17.2 x 12.1 cm)
Page 91

WYNN RICHARDS
Abstraction (Sugar Cubes and Shadows),
ca. 1922
Gelatin silver print
7¾ x 6¹/₁₆ in. (19.6 x 15.3 cm)
Page 163

WYNN RICHARDS
Woman in Shower, ca. 1932
Gelatin silver print
13⁵/₁₆ x 10⅜ in. (33.8 x 26.4 cm)
Page 24

WYNN RICHARDS
*Preparing Yarn for Weaving (National Cotton
Council advertisement)*, 1948
Gelatin silver print
9½ x 8⁵/₁₆ in. (24.2 x 21.1 cm)
Page 157

HENRY W. SHEPARD
*Angles, from the Window of the Clarence H.
White School of Photography, 460 W. 144th
Street, New York (The Morning Sun)*,
1924/1925
Satista print
9⁹/₁₆ x 7¾ in. (24.3 x 19.7 cm)
Page 82

STELLA F. SIMON
Tennis Match, ca. 1923
Platinum print
6¾ x 9¹/₁₆ in. (17.2 x 23.0 cm)
Page 130

STELLA F. SIMON
*Exhibition and Lecture Room, Clarence H.
White School of Photography, 460 W. 144th
Street, New York*, ca. 1924
Platinum print
4½ x 3⁹/₁₆ in. (11.4 x 9.0 cm)
Page 141

STELLA F. SIMON
Violin, ca. 1925
Platinum print
8 x 6¹/₁₆ in. (20.3 x 15.3 cm)
Page 99

CLARA E. SIPPRELL
*Tents and Clouds at the Hill Camp, Hanoum
Camps, Thetford, Vermont*, 1917
Gelatin silver print on tissue
4¹⁵/₁₆ x 3⅞ in. (12.5 x 9.8 cm)
Page 46

CLARA E. SIPPRELL
Still Life, Jug, and Fruit, 1920s
Platinum print
9⁹/₁₆ x 7½ in. (24.4 x 19.0 cm)
Page 94

FRANCES SPALDING
*Columns, Low Memorial Library, Columbia
University, New York*, 1922
Platinum print
4¹³/₁₆ x 3¹³/₁₆ in. (12.2 x 9.6 cm)
Page 72

EMA SPENCER
Kitten's Party (Child Study), ca. 1899
Platinum print
6¹⁵/₁₆ x 5¼ in. (17.6 x 13.3 cm)
Page 128

RALPH STEINER
Typewriter Keys, 1921
Gelatin silver print
8¹/₁₆ x 6 in. (20.5 x 15.3 cm)
Page 109

RALPH STEINER
Lollipop, 1922
Gelatin silver print
4⅞ x 3¹⁵/₁₆ in. (12.3 x 10.0 cm)
Page 113

RALPH STEINER
The Village, 1922
Gelatin silver print
4⅜ x 3⁵/₁₆ in. (11.0 x 8.4 cm)
Page 142

RALPH STEINER
After Rehearsal, 1936
Gelatin silver print
9⅝ x 7⁹/₁₆ in. (24.4 x 19.2 cm)
Page 155

KARL STRUSS
*The Landing Place, Villa Carlotta, Lake
Como, Italy*, 1909
Platinum print exposed on both sides of the
paper
5¼ x 7⁷/₁₆ in. (13.3 x 18.9 cm)
Page 47

KARL STRUSS
New York Harbor, East River, 1909
Platinum print
4⅝ x 3⅜ in. (11.7 x 8.5 cm)
Page 43

KARL STRUSS
*Queensboro Bridge, at 59th Street and the
East River, New York*, 1911
Platinum print
In presentation album for Amy Whittemore
4⅝ x 3⅝ in. (11.7 x 9.2 cm)
Page 41

KARL STRUSS
Nude Female with Fan, 1917
From *The Female Figure*
Gelatin silver print
7⅛ x 8½ in. (18.1 x 21.5 cm)
Page 23

KARL STRUSS
*Ethel Wall Struss Seated under Two
Trees*, 1921
Gelatin silver print
10⅛ x 13⅛ in. (25.7 x 33.3 cm)
Page 123

EDITH WINIFRED TAIT
Hull of Ship with Anchor, 1926
Platinum print
4⁵/₁₆ x 3³/₁₆ in. (10.9 x 8.1 cm)
Page 44

EDITH WINIFRED TAIT
Study of a Hand, 1926
Platinum print
4¹¹/₁₆ x 3¾ in. (11.9 x 9.5 cm)
Page 185

EVERETT S. TURNER
Hollyhocks, Canaan, Connecticut, 1921
Platinum print
8⅛ x 6 in. (20.6 x 15.2 cm)
Page 59

DORIS ULMANN
*Abstraction (Metropolitan Museum of Art seen
through the Greywacke Arch, Central Park,
New York)*, 1917
Platinum print with pencil
6⅛ x 8¹/₁₆ in. (15.5 x 20.5 cm)
Page 88

ACKNOWLEDGMENTS

This book and the accompanying exhibition have brought together many people who care deeply about the history of photography and who recognize the unique and unacknowledged role Clarence White and his students played at an important transitional stage.

First, Warren and Margot Coville have collected the work of Clarence White and his students for a number of years. Through their vision, and generous and enthusiastic support, this project is a reality.

Both book and exhibition benefitted from the interest, time, and energy of many individuals. For professional assistance and access to public collections, thanks to: Adrienne Aluzzo, Archives of American Art, Smithsonian Institution, Detroit; Miles Barth, International Center of Photography; James Borcoman and Lori Pauli, National Gallery of Canada; Peter Bunnell and Toby Jurovics, The Art Museum, Princeton University; Mark Burnette, Evanston Historical Society; Leslie Calmes and Timothy Troy, Center for Creative Photography, University of Arizona, Tucson; Keith F. Davis, Hallmark Photographic Collection, Hallmark Cards, Inc., Kansas City, Missouri; Virginia Dodier, The Museum of Modern Art; Lydia Dufour, Frick Art Reference Library; Elizabeth Engle and Karen Sinsheimer, Santa Barbara Museum of Art; Carl Esche, Mudd Manuscript Library, Princeton University; Patricia Fanning, F. Holland Day Collection, Norwood Historical Society; Sarah Greenough, National Gallery of Art; Hollee Haswell and Sara Vos, Columbia University; Morrison Heckscher, Metropolitan Museum of Art; Brooks Johnson, Chrysler Museum; Lionel Kelly, University of Reading, England; Barbara McCandless and Paula Stewart, Amon Carter Museum, Fort Worth; Dale Neighbors, New-York Historical Society; Kent Newman, Wallace House Foundation, Des Moines; Arthur Ollman, Museum of Photographic Arts, San Diego; Christian Peterson, Minneapolis Institute of Arts; Helen Pinkney and Dominique Vasseur, Dayton Art Institute; Earl Rogers, University of Iowa, Iowa City; Peter Simmons, Museum of the City of New York; Sara Stevenson, Scottish National Portrait Gallery; Bette Weneck, Milbank Memorial Library, Teachers College, Columbia University; and Deborah Wythe, The Brooklyn Museum.

For allowing access to unpublished documents, thanks to: Michele Bogart, State University of New York College at Stony Brook; and Patricia Johnston, Simmons College, Boston.

For personal reminiscences and access to private collections, thanks to: Helen Simmons Faye, San Diego; Hans Jorgensen, Edmonds, Washington; Ira W. Martin Jr., San Jose; Phyllis Dearborn Massar, New York; Joseph Mulholland, Mulholland Archive, Glasgow, Scotland; and Joy Weber, Santa Fe.

Dealers, commercial galleries, and auction houses also played a crucial role in understanding the history of an era. In New York City, thanks to: Bonni Benrubi; Keith de Lellis; Howard Greenberg and Kerri Springer, Howard Greenberg Gallery; Daile Kaplan, Swann Galleries; Robert Mann; and Susan Arthur Whitson, Houk Friedman. For help outside of New York City, thanks to: Joseph Bellows, San Diego; Tom Halsted and Wendy Halsted, Halsted Gallery, Birmingham, Michigan; Tom Jacobson, San Diego; and Mus and Stephen White, Stephen White Associates, Los Angeles.

For their generous hospitality in the course of research: Steve Kowalik; and Joseph, Claire, and Brian Mulholland.

For historical information, advice, and support, special thanks to: Edward and Betty Erwin, Bob Halliday, Judith Herschman, Philip Jacobs, Robert Makla, Betty Muirden, Peter Palmquist, Bill Rauhauser, Naomi Rosenblum, Billie Todd, and Pam Wilson.

The staffs at the Detroit Institute of Arts, where the exhibition originated, and George Eastman House, where this book was edited and assembled, brought together the many elements of *Pictorialism into Modernism* with care and expertise. The publisher, Rizzoli, steered the book through its production stages with faithfulness to both its form and its spirit.

These acknowledgments are written on behalf of one collector, two writers, and two institutions. We hope that all who contributed to the coming together of two essays, one book, and an extraordinary exhibition—whether named or not—accept our sincerest appreciation.

—*Marianne Fulton*